Marriage Talk

Marriage Talk

How to Communicate & With Your Spouse

Ron Woods

Deseret Book Company
Salt Lake City, Utah

The persons and incidents portrayed in this book are fictitious.
Any resemblance to actual persons or situations is coincidental.

First printing August 1988

Library of Congress Cataloging-in-Publication Data

Woods, Ron.
    Marriage talk : how to communicate with your spouse / Ron Woods.
       p.   cm.
    Includes index.
    ISBN 0-87579-151-4 : $9.95 (est.)
    1. Communication in marriage. 2. Interpersonal relations.
I. Title.
HQ734.W9375   1988
646.7'8—dc19   88-14831
                           CIP

To Zina

CONTENTS

PREFACE

"And they lived happily ever after. . . . " How simple it sounds. But while millions of couples certainly do live happily ever after, it isn't necessarily simple. Marriage takes at least as much work as any other thing of value.

When two individuals from different backgrounds—with different values, abilities, views, and interests—are combined into the intimate and all-encompassing relationship of marriage, the potential exists for considerable "chemistry."

In the best of matches, confusion, hurt feelings, and unintended, negative results are about as likely as are growth, increased appreciation, and love. Of course, it's the latter we want. But achieving these is far from automatic; real effort and constant diligence are required.

At times, the messages we send one another in a marriage are not what we intend. In the little things of daily life as well as in the crises and weightier events, the potential exists for missent or misread messages. The way we are, or think we are, is not how we're seen. Our motives are sometimes unclear—even to ourselves—or are misunderstood by our spouses. Marriage talk can be difficult!

In this book, couples are seen in numerous situations where the potential for mismatched messages occurs. In some cases, couples identify and work through the problem successfully. In others, they "talk past each other" or otherwise fail to notice how their messages are garbled. (I hope that the inclusion of unsuccessful as well as successful cases will not be seen as negative, but as realistic and instructive.)

You and your spouse may wish to read the book together and discuss the concepts that interest you most. Thought questions follow each chapter to guide and assist you in your discussions.

Achieving a better marriage takes lifelong effort. It's a continuous process—more a journey than a destination. But two dedicated people can make a fine trip out of it. With goodwill and concerted, regular work on the messages they send one another, their marriage can grow. And whether a couple is newly wedded or well into double-digit anniversaries, living "happily ever after" is a worthy and attainable goal.

CHAPTER 1

SIMPLIFYING COMPLEXITIES

Life is complex. People are complex. Relationships can be complex. Especially in marriage, where two people come to know each other intimately—where your spouse may know you better in certain ways than you know yourself—there is ample opportunity for complexities to arise in the messages you send each other.

There's a wonderful short, short story called "The Birthday Party" by Katharine Brush that illustrates this point well. A married couple sits in a restaurant finishing their meal. A waiter brings a cake with a single candle in the center and places it before the husband while the pianist plays "Happy Birthday," and other patrons applaud. The woman beams with happiness over her little surprise. But the man is embarrassed and indignant. He says something short and unkind, and the woman begins to cry. The people look away.

That's it. Three paragraphs long, half a printed page. Little plot, minimal action. But, oh, what this story tells us about human interaction.

I've often used this fictional piece in creative writing classes as an example of how simple events can reveal character. When I ask high school students to analyze the two characters in the story, nearly all of them tell me what a bad guy the husband is and what a good woman is his wife. Few of them perceive what older readers might, on further reflection: that there are other options. Life is seldom so simple as the good-guy/bad-guy formula implies. For example, an experienced and careful observer might well ask why the woman didn't realize, after living with her husband for years, what his reaction to this kind of public attention would be? Perhaps, if we were finding fault, she would also have to be labeled a "bad guy."

For our purposes, of course, the point is not to blame either party, but to recognize that the simplest things can become complex, that continual effort is required to understand others, and that support is not always a simple matter of doing for another what you might like for yourself.

Since people are complex, some things in marriage will remain complex; we'll have to live with those. Others can be understood and simplified with effort. In the following vignettes, couples find themselves faced with confusing issues that test their ability and desire to understand one another and to appreciate each other's differences. Let's see how well they manage.

THE LITTLE THINGS

Randy's story: I came home from work yesterday evening, greeted Margaret and the kids, then went to the bedroom to change clothes. Margaret followed me and stood in the doorway talking while I put my wallet, keys, and change on my dresser. I was trying to listen, but I guess my mind was still partly at work. I was thumbing through the mail while she talked.

Under the mail was the clipboard Margaret uses to write letters on. I was picking it up to see why it was on my dresser, when the edge caught my change tray. I was startled because the tray nearly flipped over and spilled coins behind the dresser, and I jerked to grab it. No damage done, but Margaret said sharply, "What's wrong?"

"Nothing." Then I added, "What's this doing here, anyway?"

"It's the aerogram to Stuart. I thought you wanted to write on it." I looked at her. She sounded angry. I didn't know why. But I suppose her anger kind of set me off.

"It isn't even addressed," I said. "I've told you, when we write to missionaries, I'll be last so I can type my part at work and mail it from there."

The next thing I knew, Margaret had grabbed the clipboard and said, "I wanted Sister Kemp to mail it to her boy. Never mind!" And, instantly, she was down the hall and out the door. I looked out the window and she was heading down the street to the Kemps.

I decided not to say a word, but I was amazed at how, after all the times I've told her, she couldn't understand that I only want to see those letters when they're ready to mail, and that I didn't need her clipboard on my dresser spilling my change tray.

Margaret's story: Last night, when Randy came home, I mentioned that Jenny wanted to sign up for flute in the fifth-grade orchestra. I could tell Randy wasn't paying much attention, and I was deciding to wait and talk to him about it later when he suddenly made that sighing, huffing sound he makes when he's disgusted about something. It really bothers me. I asked him what was wrong, and he said, "Nothing," but I saw him looking at the clipboard I'd left for him to write a few words to Elder Kemp on.

3

"What's this?" he demanded. The question caught me off guard, I guess, and made me a little upset, because, of course, he knew very well what it was. But I told him it was a letter to one of the ward missionaries.

All of a sudden, he really came back at me.

"It's not even addressed," he said. And before I could explain that I'd heard from Sister Kemp that her son had just been transferred and that I'd told her I would bring the aerogram to her to put the new address on it, Randy was going on about how he liked to write his part at work, on and on.

"OK," I said. And I took the letter right then to Sister Kemp.

We didn't say any more about it, but I couldn't believe he could get so upset and not even let me explain.

Life can be complicated, can't it? Notice how each party reacts to the other, how each one blames the other for getting angry first, how the real cause for Randy's initial response—the near spilling of the money tray—is never known to Margaret, and how the real explanation for why the clipboard is on his dresser is never clear to Randy. Notice how Randy's description of how he "jerked to grab" the money dish is perceived by Margaret as "that sighing, huffing sound he always makes when he's disgusted about something."

Perhaps what this incident illustrates best is that there are no little things. The slightest movement, sound, or look can be tinged with meaning—or can be read that way. Bells ring, red lights flash, barriers are dropped in place. Defensiveness takes over—as it did in both Randy and Margaret—and a non-event turns into an incident.

Yet, no one started out to be belligerent here. Both

parties stumbled rather innocently into the situation. If they are guilty of anything, it isn't intent.

Is life really so treacherous? Well, most of us have seen enough small matters sprout into giant problems that we'd agree the potential exists in most human encounters.

What's to be done? Is peaceful human interaction hopeless? Must we conclude that "nothin's gonna turn out right," throw up our hands, and walk away? Not at all. A great deal can be done—through thoughtful applications of charity and kindness, and through reason, sensitivity, and communication skills—to avoid problems and to successfully work through the unavoidable ones. Despair is definitely not the answer.

The first step is recognition of this fact: Relationships can be extraordinarily complex, especially between strong personalities, no matter how much two people may love and appreciate one another. Only if we accept this premise, without guilt and without blame, can we work on ways to simplify the confusions.

FORMULAS AREN'T ENOUGH

"You said you wanted to talk about something, Carol. Can we do it now? I'm about ready to go to bed."

"OK, I'm almost finished here—just five more minutes? I think Pat's about got it." She turned to her daughter, who was being tutored in sewing a hem in a dress. "Don't you, honey?"

"I think so, Mom."

Dan was reading in bed by the time Carol came into the room. "She's doing great for nine years old. She's so patient. I think she'll be a good seamstress."

"Good."

"Dan, what I want to talk about is whether to send this newspaper clipping to Charlene and

Roger. It might help them with their problem.
Read it and see if you think sending it would be
too . . . oh, nosey or something on my part."

Carol handed Dan the clipping, torn and yel-
lowed with age.

"Where did you get this thing?" he asked.

"I've had it for ages. I clipped it out of the
paper years ago, before we were married. I think
it's from an advice columnist—I don't really remember. It has good ideas—maybe somewhat
superficial."

Dan started reading. " 'Ten rules for a good
marriage.' OK. . . . "

Carol sat on the edge of the bed, waiting for
Dan to finish reading. It took only a minute. He
sat quietly for a moment, then said, "All right.
Sounds good, I guess."

"Well, shall I send it or not?"

Dan shrugged. "Oh, I suppose it can't hurt."

"Does that mean you think I shouldn't?"

"No, I'm not saying that. But . . . I don't
know."

Carol waited. "But what?"

"Well," Dan said, "I know you want to help
your sister with the problem she's having in her
marriage. And I don't think sending her and
Roger something like this would offend them.
They would expect you to want to help. That's
not the problem."

"So? What is?"

"It's just that the list—this is only my personal reaction, now—is so . . . so simplistic."

"I know, but what's wrong with simplicity,
anyway? We do most everything on here ourselves," Carol protested.

"Yes, we do quite a few of them, I noticed.

But look at some of these things: 'Never go to bed mad.' 'Say "I love you" every day.' Uh, here's one: 'Go on a date together once a week.'

"These are good things, Carol. Not one of them is bad. And it's true that we do most of them ourselves. But we're not having marital troubles. And somehow, to suggest them as solutions to people having problems in their marriage seems, like you said, superficial. Sort of like saying, 'Just do these few outward things and all the inner problems will disappear.' I don't know, I guess I think they're pretty mechanistic. Do you see what I'm saying?"

"Yes. In fact, I wondered a little about the same thing. That's one reason I wanted you to read the list."

Dan went on. "That they work for some people isn't the point. They work in those cases, like for us, because the inner feelings are right. Then going on dates and stating our love and things like that are just good reminders not to let things slip. But when there are real problems in the relationship, like there appear to be with Roger and Charlene — from what she told you — it's like telling them to just act like everything is OK and it will be. And that doesn't usually work for very long."

"That's for sure," Carol said.

"Sometimes, maybe getting the motion brings the emotion — or whatever that saying is — but not always, not by a long shot. It's sort of like telling people that if they hold home evening regularly, they'll never lose a child, without telling them that quality and approach and loving relationships are the keys — not merely going through the motions. Or that going to bed early and getting up early is guaranteed to make them healthy, wealthy, and wise."

As Dan and Carol both know, human relations can't be reduced to a matter of a few simple formulas. When people try it, they often end up pretending all is well while masking the real problems. Simple formulas and guidelines generally enhance a marriage only when the foundation is sound. If it isn't, hanging pictures on the walls won't do much to strengthen the house.

Reliance on formulas can be poor substitutes for real understanding. Therefore, Dan might even be wrong when he said that sending the list "can't hurt anything." If living by formulas keeps Roger and Charlene from learning how to discuss their real feelings, recognizing the problems in their relationship, and working toward solutions, then these "outward" formulas might actually hurt a great deal.

People needn't toss out lists and recommendations. Some of them provide wonderful suggestions for keeping love alive. But what works for one couple doesn't always work for another. Life isn't so simple. What works for every couple, though, is an attitude of wanting to find the roots of their problems, and a willingness to lovingly work toward solutions. It's an approach that sounds, at first, more complex, but eventually leads to greater simplicity by its openness and integrity.

WAYS OF LOOKING AT THINGS

Cory watched his wife, Brenda, get up from her chair beside him and start to speak. They were in the second session of a weekend marriage enrichment seminar, and the hour was entitled "Shared Insights."

Cory hadn't been too crazy about the idea of signing up, at first, but in the first hour or two, he'd come to like the group and the leader very much. The introductions made everyone feel at home, and Cory soon saw that the participants weren't necessarily there because of failing marriages, but out of a desire to grow even stronger.

Now it was time to share their feelings on various subjects. They had drawn slips of paper at random, and Brenda's topic was: "Surprises in Marriage." Cory wondered what she would say.

"I don't know if I have too much to say about surprises in our marriage," Brenda began. "I suppose we had our usual share of amazements at a few of the little things people do— like the first time I saw Cory eating pie and ice cream for breakfast."

There were chuckles from the group. "I grew up in a Cream of Wheat family, myself. If we didn't get our portion of hot cereal in us before we went out into the world each morning, we were sure we'd keel over dead before lunch. So it was really different for me to hear Cory defending as a balanced breakfast what I call dessert.

"I expected differences like that, though. I'd heard all the stories about different ways to squeeze the toothpaste, and I was ready for those things. What I didn't know was how differently people can think about basics, and how the way each of us thinks affects so many things in the marriage. I guess that was the big surprise.

"In outward things, Cory and I are much the same. We tend to like the same ways of spending time. We're both from the same church background, our families are similar—both our dads even work in the same profession—and we grew up within forty miles of this building. You'd think we'd be almost identical. And we are quite similar, in many ways.

"But we've noticed, in the fifteen years we've been married, how there are some really basic differences between us. I never would have dreamed we could be so different in our views on raising kids, politics, even religion—several major things. I think that's something young people getting ready for marriage can't fully anticipate. They haven't had enough experience with life to even know what I'm talking about."

Several in the group nodded. Then Carol went on. "But here's the neat thing. As these differences have caused us a certain amount of tension and occasional 'blow-ups,' we've been able to talk about them. We've come to the conclusion that differences are a natural and acceptable thing. Everybody is simply different from everybody else. You can go along without a problem for a long time, and then something happens that causes a reaction in your mate you can't begin to figure out."

Brenda turned to Cory. "We've learned that we can be different, yet still function well as a team. Sometimes I think maybe we even love each other more because of these differences."

There are as many ways of looking at the world as there are people. Hopefully, couples will take the time to get to know each other in as many areas as possible before marriage. But even then, they are certain to find reactions and ways of thinking in one another that will surprise them.

Besides that, we sometimes surprise ourselves; trials and new experiences change us, making us into new people. How can one know for certain what kind of parent she will be to a teenage child until she has one? How can one know how he will react to financial setbacks or serious illnesses until they happen?

People are wonderfully varied; others won't always see things as we do. But, as Brenda says, we must learn that we can be "different, yet still function well as a team." Complexity, in this sense, isn't necessarily a problem but can become a strength.

CONFLICT IS INEVITABLE

"Joyce, I tell you, I get so disgusted with myself."

Alora wasn't sure how she and her neighbor had gotten into this discussion, but it suddenly felt good to find someone to talk with about her concern. She'd gone out to move the sprinkler on the grass, had seen Joyce on her knees weeding a flower bed in her yard next door, and had gone to the fence to talk—first about the gorgeous spring weather, then about their kids. Somehow, they'd moved to how they each handled difficulties in their homes. And now, here Alora was, confessing her frustrations.

"Time and time again, I've committed myself not to get upset with Jim or the kids," she said. "To overlook things, to be a better wife and mother. And I do pretty well for a while, sometimes for weeks at a time. Then something happens, and before I know it, I'm into an argument or I've blown up over something, often minor.

"I feel bad afterward that I didn't keep my promise to myself and just be understanding and kind and give the 'soft answer.' It really disappoints me and makes me feel guilty."

"I don't mean to sound flippant, Alora," Joyce said, "but welcome to the club! It sounds to me like you're a normal human being. We've been neighbors for six years, and I've never known you to be hard to get along with. I think you're being too tough on yourself. Conflicts are as certain as this pesky morning glory in my flower beds."

"Well, Joyce, I agree that I'm too hard on myself in certain areas, and maybe this is one. But I was raised in a home where parents never had a problem with each other—at least not in front of us kids. They were both quiet people, and they simply didn't react negatively to one another. I grew up thinking that was the way to be—that it was bad to have conflicts, that good people just didn't. You know, 'If you can't say something nice . . .'

"So when I hear these modern ideas about talking out your difficulties, saying what you think, and so forth, it just goes against the way I was raised. I feel guilty that there's a conflict in the first place, let alone about feeling a need to speak my piece. So I keep quiet and live with the guilt."

The weight of self-recrimination Alora is carrying is needlessly hurting her life. Not that all of us don't experience certain reactions that need to be controlled, but Alora's expectation that she must never disagree or feel a conflict is a denial of her humanity. It's an impossible and even unhealthy demand.

Many people berate themselves because they aren't perfect. Alora goes even further. She denies herself the right to have views and feelings different from those of others.

Families are a great place to learn how to handle differing views. Alora misses this point when she equates "overlooking things" with being "a better wife and mother." The measure of Alora in either role is not in how much she overlooks or in how well she buries her feelings.

Trying to keep from feeling is a misguided effort to simplify a complex world, like trying to change the weather to avoid storms. It can't be done. Conflicts will come. The important question is how they're handled.

COMPLEXITY COMES WITH KIDS

"So, Myriam, give me a rundown. What have you and Cole been up to for the past fifteen years?" Liz had to raise her voice above the conversation of the crowd that filled the gym.

"In twenty-five words or less, right, Liz?" Myriam laughed. "Really! You show up for this reunion, after missing both the five- and ten-year ones, and expect me to remember that far back?"

"I didn't show up for the others because I was about 8.9 months pregnant both times," Liz answered with a grin. "I didn't dare travel out of state. And, to be honest, I didn't want my old high-school friends—especially boy friends—to see me in the shape I was in. But this time, I just had to come. David was great about taking care of things at home while I flew up. And, yes, I want to hear it all."

"Well, OK, you asked for it," Myriam started. "You already know about my going to college—because you started with me. I graduated, then worked for two years in D.C. for Senator White's office. That was great—but I'm supposed to be giving a summary here, so I'll move on. I want to leave time to hear about you, too.

"Next: marriage. What's funny is that after all the guys I'd dated in college and afterward—and some of them were pretty neat—I should come back to our hometown and marry Cole, the proverbial boy next door. Have you seen him yet? He's right over there talking to Mrs. Clinger,

who's still here teaching English. I never liked
Cole at all in high school—hardly noticed him.
But when I met him in Washington, it was differ-
ent. He was different, or I was, or both.

"Well, I was twenty-three then. Let's see, I've
only got nine more years to cover. Have I used
up my twenty-five words yet?"

"You're doing great. Keep going."

"Well, Cole was finishing law school and
when he graduated, we went with a firm in London.

"London! Oh, wow!"

"Yeah, it was neat. He'd specialized in inter-
national law. It was a junior position without a
lot of future, but we wanted the experience of
living abroad. And it was so much fun. He trav-
eled all the time, and I went with him a lot—
Paris, Bonn, Brussels, most of the capitals of central and northern Europe—those were the regular
places he visited almost monthly. The company
even kept an apartment in some of those places
just waiting for us.

"We made side trips all over Europe, even
the Middle East, Greece. Oh, all over. We loved
it. We stayed there for almost four years. I
worked part of the time with British Airways, in
advertising—my major—so, besides Cole's business travel, I could get us cheap tickets to almost
anyplace.

"Then, when we came back five years ago—
just in time for the tenth reunion, incidentally—
Cole went with a firm in Seattle. He's close,
now, to becoming a partner. I work for a public
relations firm, we have a nice house out across
the Hood Canal, a share in a cabin at a mountain

resort area, and Cole even flies his own plane. Wow, am I bragging, or what?"

Liz listened with great interest but with a growing anxiety that when it came her turn, the report on her life over the past fifteen years would be a little less spectacular.

She reviewed and compared as Myriam talked: By the time Myriam married—after finishing college and two years in a senator's office—Liz had already been married four years, had two children, and had dropped out of school to work while David finished.

In the next nine years—while Myriam flitted around Europe, then established herself in Seattle—Liz and David had three more children. One required access to regular specialized medical care, which limited the areas they could live in. Another showed an aptitude for music, and Liz and David spent a good deal of money on her lessons and equipment. The growing family's need for a bigger house and car—not to mention braces, sports equipment, and clothes—kept the family budget tight. There was certainly no money left for trips to Europe.

There were no regrets, Liz reminded herself, but she wondered if Myriam remembered how, when they were finishing high school fifteen years ago, the two of them had told one another of their plans to travel the world.

Let's leave Liz with her thoughts. There's no doubt about it: kids complicate things. Notice how in all of Myriam's innocent reporting on her activities, children are never mentioned. Apparently she and Cole have none.

We're not here to judge the appropriateness of a family's size, but simply to join Liz in observing that having a family does often limit certain options. The presence of children, especially in quantity, can alter things quite a bit. Most couples feel a definite budget squeeze when a two-room apartment has to be replaced with a five-bedroom house, when the Volkswagen Bug has to be traded for a three-seat station wagon, and when taking the family out for hamburgers takes as much cash as the newlyweds used to live on for a week.

Besides budget constraints, there are more subtle adjustments. At times, couples with children have moved to be closer to schools—or, in other cases, when they wanted to move, have stayed put to avoid leaving particular school boundaries. They've sought new positions to move to areas deemed better for raising kids—or turned down transfers and promotions to stay in areas they preferred for child-rearing.

The list goes on. And while this isn't a book about parenting per se, it's important to point out how children make life—and marriage—considerably more complex. On some days, parenting is about as peaceful as having a long freight train run through the middle of the house. But there are other, quieter days, and fortunately—on most of them—most couples find the rewards of parenthood more than adequate.

One troubling study recently disclosed that marital satisfaction decreased sharply for new parents while remaining stable for childless couples. One explanation is that children consume most of a couple's available time and energy; the marriage tends to get put on hold. But this need not be the case if we're on guard.

Parents may need to remind themselves, at times, that, in spite of possible desires for more freedom and money (and perhaps merely some peace and quiet), they really wouldn't likely trade away the joys of parenting. A quiet house may sound attractive—but that odd phenomenon will come to all of us soon enough. And it will surely bring with it more than an occasional longing for a return to those sometimes-hectic days of parenting — days when we were truly and intently needed.

Children definitely create complexity, but they are also capable of producing tremendous fulfillment and happiness. The challenge is to provide the emotional support children need and still prevent the marriage from suffering during the hectic child-rearing years — clearly no easy task, but not out of reach, either.

CRISES AND LOST DREAMS

Del sat alone in the dark living room, thinking. The dim glow from the night-light in the hall threw long shadows on the ceiling. The only sound was the occasional creak of a floorboard or structural beam as the house cooled and settled deeper into night.

Del had slept some, then, as was his pattern lately, awakened with a start. The green numbers on the bedside clock radio said 3:04. He'd lain still, so as not to awaken Debbie, listening to her regular breathing, getting more tense and irritated with himself by the minute. He wished he could sleep like she could. He needed his sleep. But, lately, he couldn't get through a whole night, no matter how tired he was.

Finally, at 3:20, Del slipped lightly out of bed, got a drink of water in the kitchen, and sat down on the living room sofa. No use going back until he'd calmed his thoughts.

"OK," he said to himself, "I've got to think this all through and get a handle on it." How many times he'd already "thought it all through." He'd convinced himself on each point that there was no cause for this kind of worry, but somehow it didn't help much. He still felt weighed down.

"Maybe this is just how forty-five-year-olds are supposed to feel," he thought. "The old mid-life crisis in all its glory."

He could list his bigger worries by heart; he'd done so often enough. Threatened layoff at the plant. Bad feelings between himself and Carl, his eighteen-year-old son. Feelings of failure, or at least of non-excellence, as a husband, father, employee, church member—as everything, really. And last but not least, his newest worry—Carlee's diagnosis.

Deterioration of the optic nerve. What a thing to have to tell a ten-year-old. But Carlee was adjusting quite well to diminishing vision. "I'm the one with the problem, not her," Del thought. Carlee always was a resilient one, toughened by standing up for herself as the only daughter in a family of boys. She'd handle it. And she had time to prepare—several months, at the least, to get ready for a world of darkness.

But how could a child—or anyone else—really prepare for that? How could people prepare for most of the things life might throw at them? Maybe it was only our ignorance of the future that allowed us to go on. Maybe the early settlers of the West wouldn't have made the journey if they had known the hardships they would face. Would they? Del wasn't sure.

The thought reminded him of his grandfather, Calvin Eustis Mecham, dead now twenty-four years. He'd been one of those pioneers of the west. His life had reached into the Kennedy presidency, but it had started in Arkansas ninety-six years before, way back in the 1860s. Del often

wondered how a man who had been brought
west to Idaho in a covered wagon before he was
six years old could ever adjust to the age of jets.
Grandpa had lived almost long enough to see
men walk on the moon.

Grandpa Mecham had seen a few troubles,
too, Del knew: buried two wives, lost three children in eight days to the influenza epidemic of
1916 and two others to accidents or disease before maturity, lost a home to fire, a farm to the
bank. Del knew he should feel well off by comparison, but it didn't help. Just because things
could be worse seldom made them peachy-keen.

How did Grandpa handle these things? Del
stood and turned on a lamp. In the bookcase, he
found Grandpa Mecham's journal, or—more accurately—the journal written for him by one of
his daughters, Del's Aunt Angela, when
Grandpa was in his eighties. Del had read most
of it years ago, when it was first bound and sent
to family members, but hadn't looked in it for
years now.

He thumbed through the thin volume, looking for some statement of wisdom and strength,
some formula by which to retain peace in a
world filled with surprises and difficulties. The
prose was sparse. Most events received little
commentary: "April 4, 1908: Buried little Asal today, in the grassy patch above the orchard. He
was never strong from birth, and wasted away
over the winter." Aunt Angela added details
about certain things, but in those cases, it was
usually clear she was putting her words into
Grandpa's mouth.

Del read for another few minutes when his
eyes fell on a more complete passage about the

death of another child: "Georgina was near wild over Tom's death, worse than over any of the others, maybe because he was so near manhood at nineteen years and his manner of dying so hard. After some weeks, I said to her, 'You've got to let it go now, or it's going to kill you, too. And we need you too much—the kids and me—for that to happen.'

"I told her I didn't understand these things either, and it hurt me awful bad, too, to have my boy gone. I wasn't religious, and I didn't have any answers about why it should be, or what it meant, or anything. But two things I knew. First, tough things do come in life, and, second, we can't dare let them knock us down. Life will hit us with its arrows. If we fall over and don't get right up, we're done, because other darts will find us lying there and keep us down. We have to keep walking, even in our pain, or we've got no chance.

"I said, 'Georgina, your boy is gone, you can't bring him back. The hurt will be with us for the rest of our lives. But we got to keep on living. We got to keep each other going. For Tom, if nothing else. Together, we got to build strength out of this pain.' "

The entry concluded, "It took some time—several months—before Georgina came around, but she got strong again."

Del sat for a few more minutes, then put the journal on the end table as he turned off the light and went to bed. This time, he thought he'd leave the book out, and together maybe they'd read it as a family.

Hopes are crushed, dreams shattered, crises appear in every life. Some disasters are sudden, others gradual.

Some griefs are shared, others solitary. Some problems have solutions; action and planning will alleviate their effects. Others are insoluble and must simply be borne.

But problems have one thing in common: they are seldom automatically strengthening. When we hear people talk of past troubles, we often hear them say how they grew stronger from the experience. Such talk may make us suppose that troubles have the inherent ability to make us better people. Not so. Problems can destroy as well as strengthen. Some individuals shrivel and never recover from calamity. When people grow from their problems, it's because, consciously or subconsciously, they decided to handle them in a positive way.

Like Grandpa Mecham, we all have to know two things: tough things will come, and, more importantly, we don't dare let them keep us down.

Youth is a time when life often looks all mapped out, like a straight highway to happiness. Everything is set: we'll do this first, that next, we'll marry, we'll raise kids. Experience changes that vision to one where things are not always so carefully laid out. Complexities arise. Dreams are changed, sometimes lost for good. The wide highway turns into a dimly marked and rocky path.

But just because life is different than we'd anticipated doesn't make it necessarily worse. The road may not be a six-lane freeway to bliss, but, however crooked and treacherous, it can still lead to happiness — often a deeper, more meaningful happiness than our earlier vision allowed us to even imagine. Complications then become a cause for celebration.

I read of a man who was injured while cross-country skiing alone in the mountains of California. Unable to walk, for ten days he pushed his pack on his skis ahead of him like a sled and dragged himself along behind. When he was rescued and had had time to recuperate, he said of the ordeal, "It was the greatest experience of my life," illustrating wonderfully that the key to handling adversity and complications is attitude.

Couples vary in the amount of adversity they face, but life's complications are certain to enter every marriage. How they're handled determines the outcome. Our constant efforts to simplify and understand and grow must be tempered with patience and acceptance of the trials, as well as of the pleasures of our existence.

QUESTIONS FOR DISCUSSION

Do we recognize complexity as a fact of life? Together, do we accept the view that joint efforts can help us overcome difficulties and complexities?

Are there "little things" in our marriage plaguing the relationship? Would defining and discussing them help?

Which formulas have proved useful for us? Which have, instead, covered over real needs? Have we unduly relied on formulas in place of more in-depth analyses and approaches to our problems?

Do we recognize that each of us is different from everyone else in the world, and that even in the best match, there will be a great many different ways of looking at things? Have we come to better appreciate those differences?

Do we accept the fact that conflict will arise in our relationship? Are we convinced there need be no guilt involved in having different views? Are we committed to handling differences properly, not merely covering them over?

How do we feel about the complexities brought into our lives by parenthood? Can we achieve a balance between living for ourselves and living for our children? How can we better maintain our relationship as a couple in the midst of the demands for a relationship with our children?

Have we faced crises in our lives? How have these affected our marriage? Are there specific wounds from which we haven't fully recovered? Do we need to talk about these? In what other ways could we enhance the healing process?

Can we prepare for future difficulties, in spite of not being able to predict exactly what they will be? What are the ways in which we can plan ahead, not only to survive, but to gain strength from difficulties?

EXPECTATIONS

The mailman once brought me an IRS check for $200 at tax-refund time. And I was disappointed. Another year, well after the regular refund period, I received notice of a spot audit and a check for something around $70—and was thrilled. Why the difference? Isn't $200 better than $70 any day? Well, no, not when I expected more in the first instance and nothing in the second. My expectations, not the amounts, made the difference in my reactions.

So it is with many things in life. We watch a basketball game in which a forward makes sixteen points, and we're disappointed, because he's been averaging twenty-eight points per game; our expectations fall short. Yet a substitute makes a couple of last-minute baskets and the crowd goes berserk. Why? Because he's never before done well in the clutch; our expectations are surpassed.

An Olympic athlete is disappointed at winning a silver medal. The achievement of what any of the rest of us would find beyond our wildest dreams—second-best in her event in the whole world—isn't good enough at the moment, when her whole orientation for months and years has been to win the gold.

In marriage, as in almost everything else, it's not external events but expectations that make the difference in how things are perceived. Our views and expectations color all aspects of the relationship. Growth in marriage calls for continual adjustments between expectations and reality. Marital happiness increases with each gradual narrowing of the gap between what we envision and what we have.

In the following vignettes, couples meet the disparity between expectations and reality head on.

KNOWING WHAT TO EXPECT

Colleen went to wipe her face in the bathroom. When she came back to where Don still sat in the living room, her tears had turned to anger. "But, Don, you said you'd change when we got married. You promised."

"Colleen, get real, would you? I told you I'd try. I'm not perfect, you know. You act like I haven't made any progress at all."

"It's been four years, and nothing is any different."

Don shook his head. "Colleen, you've got to lighten up on this thing. We've been over and over it. I'm never going to be perfect in your eyes. And it's not fair to hold against me something I said way back then. We were only kids."

"It isn't fair to promise somebody something and then not do it, either!" Colleen snapped.

There was a long silence before Don said, "We're just different, Colleen. We don't think the same. And you can't dictate to me. I have to be me. Back off."

It isn't necessary for us to know the specific problem these two are talking about to recognize a young couple coming face to face with reality, and not handling it very well. Right now, they're acting more like litigants than lovers. From what we've heard them say, they married young—"only kids." Also, it's clear they made a second, bigger mistake: assuming things would be better after they were married. Their third problem, according to Don, is that they "don't think the same."

Any older couple or marriage counselor could have predicted problems. When people are under twenty at marriage and especially when they show so-called "romantic" tendencies—such as expectations that everything will be better after marriage—problems are predictable. And while there are successful exceptions, the odds are against them.

Colleen and Don have been married four years. Are they aware that they have reached a difficult time in marriage? Would it benefit a young couple to know that divorce statistics peak around the fourth year of marriage? Would expecting the honeymoon to fully end at that time help them to prepare and build a solid foundation—assuming they're committed to the relationship?

Would it help them to know that the middle years of marriage—ten to thirty years after the wedding, during which the kids are growing up and leaving home—are also years when a relationship requires greater effort to keep intact?

Would people better prepare themselves if they knew what lay ahead? Would it help young people considering marriage to know that tough times may come at specific points or on specific matters? Is there value, at any age, in knowing what to expect?

The answer to these questions is probably yes. People would benefit from such information if they would pay attention to it. There is evidence that realists do better than romantics in preparing for marriage. Couples can do a great deal to adjust their youthful expectations—not to become pessimists but realists. An informed couple can become its own best support group.

We want our doctor to tell us what to expect if we come down with an ailment. A driver crossing the country wants a map showing not only his destination and the straightest route, but also the detours, delays, and road work along the way. So counselors advise us to watch for difficulties of certain kinds and at certain points in marriage. Knowing what to expect and preparing for it together can help a great deal when the road gets rough.

HER VIEW, HIS VIEW

Ned felt his anger growing as he listened to Dr. Chalmers speak about closeness in marriage. What did this have to do with him? Why had he allowed Kris to talk him into coming to a marriage counselor anyway? There was nothing major wrong with their marriage, and Ned found it embarrassing to sit in front of a psychologist and talk about his feelings for his wife. He and Kris enjoyed each other's company, they had good kids, they were doing well in life, getting ahead financially. What was the problem?

"One of the things I miss," Kris was now saying, "or feel I need, is more closeness. I don't know what to call it, but there's a sort of emptiness sometimes."

"Closeness!" Ned thought. Kris was using Dr. Chalmers's favorite word. "Good grief, we spend more time together than most couples I know. What does she want?"

"Ned, what's your impression of that?" Dr. Chalmers was asking.

Ned stifled a desire to walk out. "I don't know what it means, Kris," he said to his wife. He turned back to Dr. Chalmers. "We spend all kinds of time together. Last Saturday, for example, we worked together—the kids, too, all of us—out in the yard in the morning. Then Kris and I and two of the kids went to a campus movie in the afternoon. And that night, I went with her to a concert in town. I didn't want to, really, but I know she likes these things, and I'm willing to go.

"That particular day we spent more time together than usual, but not all that much more. We go to movies, we watch TV together, we talk about things. I think we both go out of our way to spend time with each other. I don't know any couple who spends more time together, unless they're newlyweds or retirees. We go to things together, we work together."

He turned back to Kris. "I just don't understand your concern for closeness. What is it you want? What does it mean?"

What it means is that women and men often possess differing expectations about intimacy and tend to define closeness differently. Ned is understandably hurt because he goes out of his way—not as a duty, but because he enjoys it—to spend time with his wife. Yet Kris still feels a lack of emotional intimacy. Is she demanding too much?

Recent research reveals aspects of the problem. It appears that, for many men, doing things like working in the yard or going to a movie with their wives makes them feel close. Yet, for wives, activities may not be enough. They often require intimate conversation—especially about the relationship itself—in order to feel truly close to their husbands. By comparison, women may feel they are sitting at a banquet table with their husbands, but with their own plates only half-filled.

This basic difference in expectations can lead to difficulties, but certainly not insoluble ones. Both plates can be filled to capacity.

Growth begins to occur when a wife understands that her husband enjoys her company and is fulfilled by their shared activities, and when a husband accepts that his wife may need more—the opportunity to talk in deeper ways about the relationship. Kris's frustration should be lessened when she realizes Ned isn't purposely avoiding such conversation, but that he simply doesn't know she needs it. This new openness could also be a little unnatural to Ned—as it is for many males—and Kris may need to lead the way. With effort, both spouses will ensure that they each enjoy the feast to the fullest.

DEFINING ROLES: WHO IS THE LEADER?

Anna was incredulous as she unpacked the grocery bag at the kitchen counter. "Cardamom? Cream of tartar? Thyme? Toby, why did you buy all these spices? I send you to the store for milk, and you come back with a dozen boxes of spices? Why, there are things here I've hardly even heard of."

"Sure, you have," Toby said. "Look, bay leaves, cloves, ginger . . . "

"Yes, I know about those, Toby," Anna said, rolling her eyes. "I'm not that bad a cook. But turmeric, marjoram, cumin? These are pretty exotic."

"You're not a poor cook at all, honey," Toby said. "But we're just getting started in marriage, and we need some of these things. My mom has them all. I thought they could, well, spice things up a little."

"Very funny," Anna said. "But they're so expensive. And half of them I have no idea what to do with. Dill seed?" Anna shook her head. "How much did all this cost anyway?"

"The slip's in there," Toby said as he took off his coat. "Under twenty-five dollars."

"Twenty-five dollars!" Anna exclaimed. "Good night, that's nearly a week's food money! What are we going to do for the rest of the month?"

"Oh, I don't know. We'll make it. Won't we?" After a moment, he added, "I was only trying to help out with the cooking. I thought that was our plan, to help each other in every-thing—be equals—in our marriage. I thought we were liberated."

Who's in charge of the cooking around here, anyway? Who's responsible for the food budget? These are questions that Anna and Toby haven't yet faced in their few weeks of marriage. But, from what we've observed, the moment is fast approaching when they must come to an understanding. Up until now, they've apparently operated on assumptions, some of which may require scrutiny.

Toby feels confused. He says he thought they were going to be a "liberated" couple. Certainly ours is an age when the clear-cut areas of responsibility of former eras have blended and blurred a great deal. And this has produced valuable new freedoms for both sexes. At the same time, as with any change, adjustments are required. Change has its costs.

Anna feels confused, too. Where Toby thinks he is merely helping her with her shopping and cooking needs, she may feel he is creating extra burdens for her. Not only does she now have a cupboard full of nonessential spices, but also a cupboard somewhat bare of basics—and little more food money for the rest of the month. Maybe young lovers can live on sage soup or aroma of oregano. These two will soon know.

Toby's desire for equality and sharing of work is com-

mendable. In one survey, over half of the women inter-
viewed said their husbands helped with cooking and shopping, and over 80 percent helped with feeding and
changing babies. Excellent. But what Toby and Anna will
learn is that things will go more smoothly if one of them
is primarily in charge of each major area.

Modern partnership marriages provide powerful opportunities for growth and togetherness—as long as it's
clear who is basically responsible for specific categories. A
leader is needed in most everything we do. People need
to know their roles. It's part of knowing what to expect.

As a member of a branch presidency at the Missionary
Training Center in Provo, I see missionaries arrive each
week with considerable confusion on their faces. For the
first few hours, they're familiarized with where they will
spend the next several weeks. They pay their fees, unpack,
meet their companions. By the time the branch presiden-
cies meet them at Thursday night branch meetings, they've
been in the MTC for a little over twenty-four hours, and
they still look a bit lost. But after branch meeting, they are
introduced to their teachers in the classrooms. By the time
we see them again on Sunday, they look much more at
home. Friday and Saturday have taught them their routine.
Their role is now more clear to them. People need to know
where they fit.

Toby and Anna are like those missionaries; they're still
learning where they fit. When they work it out, they may
decide that Anna will make the basic decisions about how
to spend the food money, and that Toby will provide the
leadership on something else. Note that this doesn't imply
simply dividing up the tasks and going back to an era when
the work in the home all belonged to women. Instead, it
means being clear about leadership responsibilities. Too
many cooks really do spoil the broth.

Toby can and should still help with cooking, cleaning,
shopping. But he mustn't undercut Anna's responsibil-

ity—if that's who they decide should "own" this particular task—to feed them through the month on a finite amount of money.

EXPECTED SUPPORT

"Hi, how'd it go?" Larry asked. He was in bed early, propped up on his pillow against the headboard, trying to get in some reading while he waited for his wife to come home.

"OK."

There was something in Kathy's tone. Larry looked up from his magazine. She wasn't looking at him. He let it go, and went back to reading. As Kathy got ready for bed, Larry noticed her quick movements and uncharacteristic silence, signs he had come to read as markers of agitation. He waited until she'd finished writing in her journal before he asked, "Is something wrong?"

It took her a moment to answer. Then with a sigh, Kathy said, "I'm being silly. It's no big thing; I just wanted you to come."

"Oh," Larry said simply. He put down his magazine. It all came back to him now. He should have seen how important this evening was to Kathy, but he honestly hadn't figured it out until this moment. At dinner, she'd said she was going to the ward building later to practice the organ, and if anybody wanted to come, they were welcome.

"Why, mom?" one of the kids had asked. "Just to hear you practice?"

"Well, I've got the Bach fugue down pretty well now, the one that seemed impossible when Dr. Brewster first assigned it to me." She said it like a question, and Larry nodded. He knew that

Kathy's organ teacher, a friend who was a professor at the university, kept her challenged by
giving her difficult works. She was good and she
practiced hard, but she wasn't always confident
of new pieces.

Kathy went on. "And the number I played in
church a couple of weeks ago. I've got that one
really perfected now—like I should have had it
then. So, I thought somebody might like to come
and hear me play those two—a little mini-concert
just for us."

One of the kids mentioned how cold it was in
the church on a week night this time of year. The
conversation drifted, and no more was said until
right before Kathy left. Larry recalled her coming
to him about eight o'clock to say she was walking over to the church now. She'd mentioned
again that he could come "if he wanted to."

"When you come, I'll play those numbers
and then go back to my other practicing," she'd
said. "You wouldn't have to stay."

"OK," he'd said. "Lee wants help with his
homework, though."

That's about all Larry could remember of the
conversation, but it was enough to make clear
now—though it was wasn't clear at the time—
that Kathy had really wanted to play her numbers for the family tonight, and had got her
hopes up about their attending.

"I didn't realize," he said. "I got busy helping Lee, and pretty soon it was past eight-thirty.
Geneal asked if we were going, and I told her it
was a little late now, past her bedtime, and there
would be other times we could go hear you. I'm
sorry, honey. I didn't realize how important it
was to you to have us on this particular night."

"I don't know why it was. I guess I just got
to expecting it."

Kathy is feeling guilty for "needing" her family's support, and Larry is feeling the same for not sensing her need
better. But no one need feel guilty here. These things happen in life, and they are often no one's fault.

Kathy was not demanding too much. Like a child of-
fering a gift to a friend who disdains it, she simply wanted
to share with her family and was hurt when they didn't
seem to want what she had to give.

Larry, on the other hand, wasn't being callous. He saw
Kathy's request as a casual invitation, and had no idea that
she had come to see the evening as more than merely
another weekly practice session. He didn't read Kathy's
expectations accurately.

If Larry and Kathy can continue to talk about the matter
openly and honestly, things will come out fine. But both
parties must be careful that one or the other doesn't end
up accusing.

This is a matter of failed expectations, not deliberate
rejection. It need not mean that Larry doesn't support
Kathy's organ lessons. Sometimes people read far too
much into solitary incidents. One misconception doesn't
start a trend. Kathy needs to recognize that.

Larry's job, on the other hand, now that he's got the
message, is to arrange to attend Kathy's next practice session.

If couples can openly discuss what really matters to
them, they won't feel unsupported when spouses have
varied interests or simply don't get the message.

MIND-READING

"I appreciate your calling, Sister Best," Lora
Jean said into the phone. "But, no, I guess we
won't be going this weekend." She paused to lis-

ten, then said, "Oh, I suppose there's a chance
we still could, but tomorrow's the deadline, isn't
it? And Grant hasn't said a word about it." She
paused again.

"Well, yes, I could mention it. But . . . well,
we'll see. We'll let you know. For now, though,
you'd better mark us as not going. Thanks
again."

Lora Jean put down the phone with a sigh.
How she'd love to go on the temple trip with the
ward. But, in spite of the possibility she'd held
out to Sister Best, she knew she and Grant
would not be going. He wasn't much for over-
night trips, and she wasn't about to ask him to
take her. He ought to know by now how much
she liked things like that; she'd made that clear
years ago when they were first married. But
she'd also decided long ago that she wouldn't
beg; if he really cared enough for her, he would
perceive her interest and ask. He seldom did.

Five minutes later, Grant came in the door.
"Not a word," Lora Jean promised herself.

"Hi, Lor," he called from the front door.

"Hi, honey, how was your day?" Lora Jean
asked as she came to kiss her husband.

"OK, I guess," Grant said. "It's been a heavy
week. A very heavy week."

"Oh."

No more was said as Lora Jean went back to
dinner preparations and Grant went down the
hall. "She's not interested in my week," he
thought. "I give her all these clues about my
heavy load at work, and they just pass right over
her."

Here is a couple with an expectation problem of the
first order. Each of them seems to demand mind-reading
from the other.

Notice how Lora Jean won't tell Grant of her interest in the temple trip because she feels he "ought to know by now." Note how Grant won't disclose more of his troubles at work; he gives her "all these clues" and assumes she isn't interested when she doesn't ask for details. Mind-reading is apparently a required skill for success in this marriage, and neither Lora Jean nor Grant is very adept at it.

Yet if we could pry open Grant's head and look into his mind, we would see that he supposes Lora Jean not to be interested in the temple trip—since she hasn't said anything at all about it. He had thought she would, and had actually talked himself into going this time if she wanted to, but she's never mentioned it. So he won't either.

Inside Lora Jean's mind, we would see her reason for not asking Grant about his work when he acts downcast. She simply figures he's had enough problems all day and doesn't want to talk about them at night. After all, she's right there and available, yet he only says, "It's been a heavy week." He must not want to talk about the details, she thinks, so she doesn't ask.

Here we have the sad case of two people of good intent appearing to each other to be uninterested and uncaring. And all because they demand mind-reading of one another.

Communication is tough under the best of conditions. But when people expect others to read their thoughts, it becomes nearly impossible.

Soon a spouse starts to attribute bad motives—a lack of caring—to his or her partner, as Grant and Lora Jean did: "If he really cared . . ." and "She's not interested . . ."

Mind-reading is a great stage trick, but it's only that—

a trick, an illusion; off the stage, in real life, it can't be done. In marriage, partners must tell one another how they feel.

SPECIAL EVENTS

Evelyn was hanging up the living room phone when Leland came back from the bedroom where he'd been on the extension.

"Well, Mrs. Knowles," Leland said to his wife, "I suppose now that you've heard what it's like to be married to a romantic—and a rich one, too—you'll probably want to turn me in."

"Turn you in on what?" Evelyn snorted. "A young thing I'd have to train up? Besides, I don't reckon they take trade-ins of your vintage, now, do they?"

"I might be worth a great deal—as an antique. Don't underestimate."

Leland and Evelyn had just finished talking to their third daughter who'd called from out of state to report on her anniversary present. "Our tenth, you know," Pat had told her folks. Leland hadn't known, out of long habit of purposely not paying much attention to dates and events. "And guess what?" They couldn't. "Taylor bought me a 280Z."

"A what?"

"It's a car, mother—white and silver, fast, and gorgeous."

"And paid for?" Leland whispered on the extension.

"This must be a pretty good connection, dad. I heard that," Pat laughed. "None of your beeswax. And what's a practical thing like money got to do with romance and anniversaries and love, anyway?"

"Not a thing, I guess," Leland answered. "Congratulations. And tell my wealthy son-in-law my birthday is coming up. I could always use one of those Z-80-whatevers to park beside the old Buick—which I would gladly let your mother keep just to herself. I'll take fire-engine red, with a loud stereo."

After they'd hung up and gone through the routine about Leland's trade-in value, he shook his head and said, "A car for an anniversary. It's a different world now, momma. I've just been thinking, and I can't remember the last time I bought you a real anniversary present."

Leland was quiet for a moment, looking at the figures on the TV screen, silent since the phone call. "Course, we've only had forty-seven of 'em to practice on."

"Now, listen here, you. Don't start gettin' silly on me," Evelyn said. "You always remembered our anniversary."

"Oh, yeah, I remembered it, all right. But I didn't buy you any cars. Usually didn't buy you so much as a soup ladle."

"I didn't need anything, Leland," Evelyn said. "I was happy. Still am, too." She looked at her husband. "This is bothering you, isn't it?" she asked.

"Ah," he said and waved his hand.

"All right, Leland Knowles," Evelyn started. "I'll tell you how it was with us. First off, we didn't have money for cars for presents."

"Right about that."

"And second—and you listen careful to this, or I *will* trade you in—you didn't *need* to do big things on anniversaries and birthdays and such. It just wasn't necessary."

Leland looked at her. "Meaning what?"

"Well, I'll tell you. The way I was raised, birthdays and Christmas and things like that—graduations, Easter—were really important in our family. Daddy would save all year to get us something nice. And we loved it. It helped us feel we were special to him and mother.

"You were raised different, I think. No extra money at your house, for one thing. But, besides that, I noticed, when I first got to know your people, they just didn't do much with those events.

"And when we first married, I had a little trouble getting over my expectations, I admit. Our first anniversary, I remember, you brought me a handful of flowers you'd picked on the way home. That was that. I hope I didn't show it, but I was disappointed. It took a little adjustment for me to understand your style."

Leland was looking intently at his wife, as she went on. "But—and here's the point—by the second anniversary, I didn't need presents anymore. And you know why? Because I'd come to see that you didn't wait for dates on the calendar to make me feel special. You showed me in the little things, as the years went along. I saw it with the way you treated the kids, and I saw it with me. You gave me what I needed, Leland Knowles, and don't you ever doubt it."

Our expectations about holidays and special events are pretty deeply ingrained. What newly married couple hasn't been surprised, perhaps amazed, at varying approaches and emphases about Christmas, for instance? How much preparation time is involved, how much money is spent, even how quickly or in what order or disorder the packages are opened—these can become important issues. Spouses may at first feel they've married someone from a different planet. "Doesn't everyone do Christmas the way my family did it?" we ask.

Events like Christmas and other traditional family holidays provide stability and bring back memories, usually happy, of childhood. Any tampering with them alarms us. But, in time, couples create their own new traditions—which, in turn, become "gospel" to their own offspring.

What the story of Evelyn and Leland illustrates most clearly is that it's intent, not procedure, that's important. Leland showed his love for his wife and family more frequently than just on the annual events. Although he didn't make a big deal of birthdays and anniversaries, he did make a big deal of people.

IMAGES VS. REALITY

It was lunch time at the print shop. The presses were stopped, the din diminished for the moment. Most of the crew of nine sat around a long table with their lunch boxes or paper bags.

"What's this we hear, Jody?" asked Terry.

"It's true," Jody said. "I'm taking the big step. We're looking at rings tonight."

"Great. Congratulations," Terry said. "You've gone with the poor guy long enough; it's about time you finally got around to asking him."

There was a chuckle around the table. "Yeah, he was a tough one," Jody said to further laughter, since everyone knew her fiancé had first proposed to her nearly a year ago, and she'd put him off. In the eighteen months Jody had worked part-time at the print shop, she'd learned to go along with the good-natured ribbing the permanent crew of three men gave each other and the college-age part-timers.

"Ah, you're too young anyway," Beck teased. "Only twenty-three, aren't you?"

"Yep, only. A few years ago, twenty-three seemed ancient as a marrying age, but the older I got, the more I wanted to be sure."

"Not a bad idea," Beck said.

"Wish I'd been as careful," Parker said. His comment quieted the group. Parker had been divorced for several years.

"Well," Jody said finally, "what advice do you have for me, gentlemen?"

"Ask Terry," Beck said. "He's been married the longest. Besides, he's the foreman."

"That's right," Terry said. "And that gives me prerogatives."

"Yes, master," Beck said with a mock bow that put his forehead on the table momentarily.

"Take things a day at a time, I guess," Terry said. Jody nodded.

"And," Terry continued, "there is another thing I think is important. Oh, I guess there are lots of things, if you get me started, but there's one that's pretty crucial. Learning this one took me about ten years of married life. And it's hard to explain.

"The simplest example is when the guy expects his new bride to cook like his mother. That one is pretty easy. We're supposed to know better than to make comparisons like that."

People nodded.

"But what about when we hold up our spouse against a vague mental image of what a wife or husband is supposed to be? I think most of us have some romantic, idealized image of what marriage is—and that's good, to an extent, because it makes us work at making things better. Yet it's unfair to find fault with people because they don't fit this false notion of reality.

"My main problem with this was in expecting my wife to always be understanding and patient with the children, no matter what, just because that's what I thought mothers were supposed to be like. Then when she occasionally showed herself to be human—blam, there went my image. And instead of trying to understand, I tended to condemn.

"I guess that's about it, Jody. I say it took me ten years to learn because there are so many subtleties that make it hard to notice and identify."

Terry makes an important point. How many relationships have foundered because one party has insisted that his spouse be like an image in his mind. Youth, especially, often carry a romanticized ideal of marriage that can be harmful to the relationship because it doesn't allow for real people but only for perfected beings (most of whom are in pretty short supply at any given moment).

Perhaps we should look at it like this: What we properly aim for in ourselves can be too much to demand of others. For example, when we try to never be petty, unbiased, or judging, we set up a worthy goal to work toward. But when we demand such perfect behavior of a spouse, we set up impossible standards and end up being a judge. We then can't see past the faults to the good. We're like the blind men describing the elephant—we perceive only selected portions instead of the whole critter.

Perfection is not a reasonable standard for a mate. Our spouse comes to sense the impossibility of pleasing us and feels like a failure, thereby beginning a cycle of self-defeating, defensive behaviors that will harm the relationship.

We must aim for the best and work for it together, yet

not demand that a spouse fit a preconceived image of perfection. When we do that, we carry expectations with a built-in certainty of failure.

Just as our self-expectations influence the kind of person we can become, positive expectations of a spouse can help him or her become a better person — if we couple them with patience and love. On the other hand, we can harm the relationship greatly if we demand conformity to impossible standards. Expectations are a two-edged sword that play a vital role in the development — or the destruction — of marriage and of individuals.

QUESTIONS FOR DISCUSSION

No matter how many years we've been married, are there probabilities of trouble we can prepare for in the future? Does knowledge of these predictions help us avoid them?

Do we agree on the amount of emotional intimacy we wish to share? Do we know how to talk about our relationship?

Are there areas of our household or our relationship where things become confused because it isn't clear who is in charge? Do we need to better define certain areas of responsibility?

Are there areas where one of us feels unsupported? How could we better support one another and yet have time for personal interests that needn't always be shared?

Are we guilty of expecting mind-reading from our spouse? Do we ever think, "If he/she really cared . . . " How can we be more open in our communication to avoid the demands of mind-reading?

How much in agreement are we on emphases and approaches to holidays and special events? Do we, in one way or another, make the people around us feel important?

How are we at accepting reality in one another? Do we expect our spouse to match an idealized notion of what a marriage partner is? How can we be more realistic and accepting and yet not give up encouraging the best in one another?

CHAPTER 3

COMMUNICATION

"As long as people keep talking, there's hope of solving any problem." This maxim shows the value of communication in handling day-to-day problems and in avoiding future ones. Couples who communicate come to work as a unit in solving problems, rather than as two individuals. They feel the support of one another in their decisions, and their love grows because of it.

Besides solving and preventing problems, communication in marriage provides opportunities to share joys and sorrows, intimacies and deep feelings, love and respect, beyond any other contacts most of us have. If we think of a spouse as a true friend, this sharing will seem natural and desirable. There are few more basic components of a successful marriage than the sharing of feelings.

However, some couples have built-in radar-detectors, so to speak, to deflect inquiries into their feelings. They fear intimacies. And fear builds walls.

Many people are not natural "disclosers." They have great difficulty freely revealing their inner feelings. But even they can learn to do more of it and to enjoy the results. First, they must want to change. They need to recognize that things will go better in the relationship when they communicate honestly. When the messages sent in a mar-

riage show acceptance, support, and love, happiness results.

The stories in this chapter illustrate the joys as well as
the difficulties of honest, open communication.

DON'T FORGET TO TALK

Brian and Joni have been married for fourteen
years. They are a typical American couple:
They've moved six times and have three children, two cars, a house and a mortgage, a cat,
and two goldfish. Brian works for a public utility,
and Joni works half days as the attendance clerk
at a nearby high school. Their marriage is also
typical in many ways: They get along well, love
each other, go out of their way to help one another, spend time with their children, and try to
work through difficulties.

Their busy schedule is typical of many modern, young families. Let's look at, say, last Tues-
day:

6:45   Brian arises, showers, shaves, and
dresses for work
7:10   Joni arises and showers
7:30   Brian makes toast, microwaves an egg,
and greets the kids who are now getting up
7:30   Joni eats a piece of toast and prepares
cooked cereal for the children
7:40   Brian leaves for work, followed at 8:10
by the children leaving for school
8:30   Joni drops her four-year-old off at the
baby-sitter's on her way to work
5:30   Brian comes home. Joni has been home
since noon, and the kids since about three
o'clock. Joni is cooking dinner. Brian visits with
the kids, helps a little with dinner, and watches
part of the news on TV.

6:00   Dinner

6:45   Dishes and cleanup, evening chores

7:00   TV

8:00   TV off, kids doing homework, four-year-old in bed

9:30   Kids to rooms, Joni at the kitchen table catching up on family letters, Brian reading the newspaper in the living room, then working on a home-repair project and occasionally a little paper work brought home from the office

10:00   Joni and Brian watch part of the TV news

10:30   To bed, a few minutes of reading

Wednesday's schedule was identical until after dinner. At 7:00, Joni went to a reading-group discussion while Brian watched TV with the kids until 8:30. Joni came home at 9:25. She and Brian discussed the review briefly, but since he hadn't read the book and was in the middle of family budget calculations, his interest wasn't very deep. Joni started on next month's assigned book while Brian finished his budget work and read the paper. He watched the news while she continued to read. At 10:40, they went to bed.

If we looked at each day of the week, we would see a similar schedule, with a few evenings taken up with church meetings or social events. All in all, not a terribly stressful schedule; most people would find it pretty relaxed and comfortable.

Nothing in the schedule suggests a problem in Joni and Brian's marriage. They talk, they enjoy time with their children, they spend time together every day. But if we look closely, we see that they spend much more family time than couple time. They don't seem to talk in any great depth as a couple. They don't sense a need to, perhaps.

The question might be: Are they growing together, growing apart, or holding their own? Are they keeping in practice at talking so they feel in contact, as if they really know one another?

If talking is done regularly, then, when important matters come up, they can be discussed without having to build a framework for discussion each time or without feeling awkward. Couples who talk about small problems daily find coping with the occasional big ones easier.

And where will couples find the time to spend together? The answer is that they won't find it—they'll have to create it. It's as simple—and as difficult—as that. It's not a matter of how much time is available; it's a decision. An important one.

HOW WE TALK

"Oh, I'm so frustrated," Diane said.

"What's up?" Reed asked.

"I came from shopping a few minutes ago, right? Well, I unloaded my sack of groceries onto the counter and stove top, hung up my coat, and went back to put things away to find one of the loaves of bread ruined. Melted plastic all over the burner—which someone left on.

"I didn't know the burner was on when I unloaded the groceries. But I should have. When Kari cooks, she leaves the stove on about half the time."

Reed started to speak, but Diane went on. "And it's about the third thing today! First, she used my sewing table—which is fine, except she leaves it a mess. I've asked her and asked her to leave things as she found them.

"Then, when I cleared up lunch, she'd put the wrong lid on the honey jar, one that didn't fit. She denied it, of course. So when I picked up

48

the jar, it spilled on the table. I caught it quickly,
but these things are frustrating, you know?
You'd think she'd be old enough to start thinking
a little. She is eighteen, after all. The burner
really is the last straw."

Reed said, "Well, I guess I'm in the habit of
looking at whether a burner is on before setting
anything on it."

"Oh," Diane snapped. "So it's my fault.
Well, I didn't know we were talking about me.
I'm not perfect, but what does that have to do
with Kari's irresponsibility?"

We've observed here a case of spouses talking "past"
one another. In its simplest terms, here is a summary of
the situation: Diane is frustrated over a series of incidents
with her daughter. Reed offers a response to how the
problem might have been avoided. Diane feels blamed.
Reed dislikes having his suggestion rejected. They have
failed to communicate.

Another way to state it is this: Diane is venting frustration over repeated problems with her daughter. Reed
offers a solution to future problems but gives no support
to Diane's present concern. Reed doesn't mean it as such,
but the message Diane receives is that he is rejecting her
feelings.

Let's analyze the situation. Reed's answer is, in a sense,
quite reasonable. Every cook has, at one time or another,
left a burner on. Therefore, in the interest of safety, others
in the family could conceivably train themselves to watch
for hot burners by glancing at the stove controls occasionally, especially when setting things on the burners.

While Reed does provide a solution to future problems,
he doesn't make Diane feel better. What she needs at the
moment is someone to say something along the lines of,
"Those things must be frustrating." Then, after that, he

may go on to say, "And you're right: Kari does have a problem. How can we help her? And how can we avoid future burner problems?"

Presented after his acceptance of Diane's feelings, Reed's statement about looking out for hot burners would have been taken as a helpful safety suggestion. Presented before letting Diane know he understands her frustration, Reed's idea is as out of place as would be those of a police officer lecturing auto accident victims as to future safety considerations before he offers them first aid.

Of utmost importance is a consideration of not only what the speaker is saying, but what he or she is feeling. Without that attention, talking past each other will likely become a pattern, and meaningful discussion will cease in a marriage.

How marriage partners talk is vital. And order does matter. First aid has to come first: Feelings, then solutions.

SEEING THE OTHER POINT OF VIEW

"Here's the place," Donna said, and Mark turned into the driveway. "I hope this doesn't last long. I hate to leave the baby."

"Don't worry about it. Have a good time," Mark said. "This is about the last possible shower of your old high-school friends, isn't it?"

"Yes, I think so. They're nearly all married now, those still in town," Donna said. "You won't need to pick me up. I'll catch a ride with one of the girls." She leaned across the baby seat and gave Mark a kiss, then squeezed her two-year-old. "Bye-bye, sugar. Mommy will be back soon."

"Any special instructions?" Mark asked.

"No. Just a diaper before bedtime, no later than eight o'clock these days." She reached for the door handle. "But Mark, be nice to him. You know how you're sometimes gruff. You scare him."

"Be nice!" Mark retorted. "I'm his dad! He just doesn't respond as well to me because I don't spend as much time with him as you do."

"No, it's because he thinks you're mean. He can see by your face when you're upset with him."

"Because you show him by your reaction that I'm the bad guy when you come and rescue him from me! Just because I do things differently."

Let's end this unfortunate scene by letting Donna get to her party. Mark will go home and fume. Obviously, these two have a problem to work out. It's an interesting case, since both of them were presented with new information—another point of view—but neither wanted to accept it. Mark felt accused, Donna protective.

And while we don't know the facts—only their report of the facts—it appears that Donna thinks her husband is too gruff, and that Mark thinks the problem is that he isn't around the baby enough to be as easily accepted as Donna, who spends all day with him.

Both may have a point. Maybe Mark isn't aware of rough behavior that, to a two-year-old, could come across as frightening. It's a pretty common problem. And maybe Donna isn't aware of her own reaction in the baby's presence that may add to the problem. Her "rescue" of the baby from his dad could be the real problem.

We can learn from this experience how easily two people can reject each other's viewpoint without really hearing it, like two bands marching past each other on a parade field, bugles blaring, drums pounding to their own beat. If Donna and Mark can talk further about the problem later, they may come to see that both have a point. Such an approach will obviously be in the interests of their baby and any future children.

THE ANSWERS WE GIVE

One Saturday in late November, Keith came into the house from an errand to town to find pictures of pilgrims, turkeys, and family scenes taped to the kitchen wall.

"Ann Marie!" he called.

"Yes?" she answered from the living room.

"Have you seen what the girls did to my kitchen wall?" Keith wailed.

"No, what?" Ann Marie said, as she hurried to the kitchen. She looked around but saw no cause for alarm. "What do you mean?"

"Why, these pictures pasted all over the paint."

"Oh, those?" Ann Marie said. "Those are Thanksgiving decorations they made at school. The way you were yelling, I thought they must have put them up with spikes or something. It's only masking tape. It comes right off."

"Oh, good grief," Keith groaned. "Ann Marie, don't you remember how this paint didn't stick very well when I put it on? It rubbed off just by cleaning, if we weren't careful. And now you've let them put tape all over it? The tape will come off, all right, and so will the paint."

"No, I didn't remember that, but . . . "

"Because you weren't the one who did the work to put it on!" Keith protested.

"But," Ann Marie said, angry at being interrupted and accused, "as I was saying, the paint is starting to look so shabby anyway, it didn't occur to me that taping on a few drawings would hurt anything. Where are the girls supposed to put their decorations?"

"I don't know, Ann Marie," Keith said. "I

guess when I was growing up, we just didn't
tape things to the walls."

"Maybe that's why, after fifteen years of marriage, we own so few paintings and wall coverings," Ann Marie said.

Sometimes the answers we give one another are
anything but helpful. "Because you weren't the one who
did the work to put it on," says Keith to Ann Marie.
"Maybe that's why we own so few paintings and wall
coverings," Ann Marie says to Keith.

Both of these comments are meant to hurt rather than
to communicate—like dart throwers who forget the target
and start tossing the sharp projectiles at each other. Keith's
dart is a quick response to remind Ann Marie of how
thoughtless she was with "my kitchen wall," as he calls
it. While his concern may be understandable, his way of
communicating it is not acceptable.

Ann Marie's remark is equally inappropriate. It moves
the discussion from the current concern to a new subject—
why the house has fewer wall hangings than she feels
necessary. This completely ignores Keith's feelings about
the paint and charges him with being uninterested in art
because his parents didn't allow tape on the walls—a pretty
big leap in logic. Sparks will surely follow such an accusation.

Both Keith and Ann Marie failed to listen to one another
fully. Keith's key failure was at the point where he interrupted Ann Marie to imply lack of concern and poor judg-
ment on her part because she hadn't done the painting,
when, in fact, she felt she had perfectly good reasons to
allow the pictures to go up.

Ann Marie's chance to salvage the conversation was
lost when, instead of hearing Keith's real message—his
concern about the paint—she disregarded his feelings and
broadened the issue to one of no wall hangings—all Keith's
fault.

What could have been done to keep this conversation from disintegration? At any of several points, either person could have become a listener, reflecting what was being said. "So, you feel that . . . " "You seem to be saying . . . " Phrases like these tell people that we're listening, not judging. Then, after we're sure we know what the other person feels, we can proceed to state our own feelings.

Even when a conversation has moved to the point this one has, with hurt feelings on both sides, one or the other partner can still say, "Let's back up. I want to hear what you're saying before I comment. Can we go back over your feelings once more?"

It's vital that either party—whoever thinks of it first— feel obligated to ask the right questions. Sometimes people let their pride get in the way: "She started it, so let her listen to me." Wrong, wrong, wrong. Either party can and must do the right thing. Loving listening will go a long way toward cementing relationships.

CUTE RESPONSES

Darlene was in the middle of a story her sister Faye had told her about an encounter with a co-worker.

" . . . And so, Jan is really wrought up, by now. And she says, 'Faye, this is really bothering me.' And Faye says to her, 'Well, it isn't bothering me, dear,' and walks away." Darlene chuckled to herself. "I guess the look on Jan's face was just too much. Faye thinks she really made a point."

"A point about what?" Spencer asked.

"Oh, about not making such a big deal of things, you know, and always having to talk everything out. It drives Faye crazy."

"Reminds me," Spencer said, "of the time old Slade Embley—you remember I told you

about him, how he was always going on about
the way movies and TV and nearly everything
else were corrupting us all—well, one day in the
lunchroom, he was haranguing me about something, and I said, 'Slade, if we were all as righ-
teous as you, the world would have no troubles
at all, now would it?'

"It shut him right up for quite a few days."

Such cute responses. Such powerful "last words." Such
effective conversation-enders. The ultimate punch lines.
Some people love them. They use them, not as communication tools, but as weapons—to put us in our place, to
tell us that our views are worthless and that we're pests
for having feelings about things.

"Faye thinks she really made a point." Oh, she did.
She made the point that she isn't interested in what Jan
thinks and that people with concerns had better not bother
Faye with them. Spencer made a point, too: that Slade
could take his opinions elsewhere.

Now, we don't know Jan, and we don't know Slade.
Maybe they really are pests. Maybe their views are weird,
indeed. But they're also people. And if they need to be
told to back off, they can be told in kind ways. Words
weren't meant to be bludgeons.

Without starting wars, nations can, when they try, tell
other nations when they think a policy stinks. Similarly,
people can be told anything—anything—if they're told in
the right way.

In a marriage, the cute response is divorce-fodder. A
husband or wife who uses the sharp retort or clever answer
in place of listening and discussing will build a wall of fear
and distrust that may be nearly impossible to tear down.

EMOTIONS

It all seemed to happen in slow motion. The
other car appeared out of nowhere, coming

straight at them—a sleek, green, deadly missile.
At the wheel of the station wagon, Wayne knew
instantly they were certain to be hit. His foot,
more than his mind, sensed that speeding up,
not braking, was necessary. As his cerebrum
caught up with his instinct, he knew the reason:
being hit further back on the rear fender would
certainly be better than broadside on his door.
Karen, belted in beside Wayne, made a sound of
some kind—she couldn't remember later whether
she spoke words or just yelled—and pointed at
the oncoming car. She saw the startled look on
the face of the young driver as he realized too
late the certainty of a crash. His brakes screeched
and he yanked the wheel to the right, but there
was no doubt in Karen's mind it would not be
enough.

The jolt was fierce and the tug on the seat
belts made clear how valuable they were. When
the noise stopped, Wayne shook his head to
clear it. His glasses were gone, and he found
them down between the seat and the door,
neatly folded as if he'd placed them there himself. With them back on, he saw that his station
wagon had spun 180 degrees and slid up against
the curb, facing the opposite direction, the en-
gine still running. He turned off the ignition.

"Whoa," Wayne breathed. "Are you all
right?" Karen looked fine, other than being a
little pale.

"Oh, I think so," she said. "You?"

"I hit my shoulder on the door, but I'm OK."

They looked through the windshield at the
green sports car, its hood sprung, slanted across
the intersection. The young driver got out,

glanced their way, and went to examine the front of his car.

"That was a stop sign," Wayne said. "He went right through it."

"It's a good thing he hit us where he did," Karen said, "And not a few feet further forward." Her voice was shaky.

Wayne went on like he hadn't heard. "We had the right-of-way and he went right through the sign." His voice was rising. Suddenly, Karen sobbed aloud.

The sound startled Wayne. "Are you OK?" he asked.

Karen's face crumpled. "Oh, yes. . . . Just scared. I'm fine. I need to cry a little, I guess."

"Well, I'm gonna find out what that dummy thinks he's doing, running a stop sign like that," Wayne said sharply. He grabbed his door handle. "Stupid little creep."

Same incident, different emotions. A story like this reminds us of how differently two people can react to the same external event. Both Wayne and Karen are naturally upset by the accident, but Wayne's feelings come out as anger, Karen's as tears. Of course, neither of these responses is necessarily more correct, reasonable, or better than the other. They are simply emotional releases, part of our humanity.

Some people reject emotions on principle. They feel they get in the way of logic and reason. Perhaps they do. (One might also wonder whether logic and reason are clearly the absolute pinnacles of life, though.)

Whether or not emotional responses are always helpful misses the point: Emotions are part of us. As well might we try to reject our pancreas or our liver; emotions are simply built in.

Having emotions isn't wrong; how they're handled and what they do to other people sometimes is. If couples can learn to express their emotions honestly, without blame and without guilt, their communication will bear fruit: they will understand one another—and themselves—better.

TOO MUCH COMMUNICATION

Spouse A, looking out the kitchen window, agitated: "I'm feeling really angry, and I'm going to spill it, like they say to. You agreed with me a while back that, when you worked in the yard, you wouldn't leave the tools and the stack of pulled weeds heaped on the lawn. But I can see from here you didn't mean to keep your word. That hoe out there was there night before last. And the pile of weeds has probably turned the grass yellow by now."

Spouse B, getting up from the table to look out the window: "Oh, boy. I asked Len to—"

Spouse A, very agitated: "Not another of your excuses. I see the same pattern over and over. You never do what you say you will. It's like you try to make me upset. I work to keep the place looking decent—"

Spouse B, now agitated also: "Hey, you're not the only one who does anything around here. You ought to feel grateful somebody pulls the weeds in those flower beds. You certainly never get around to it."

Is somebody carrying a referee's whistle? Let's stop the action right now before things get any worse, which they certainly will, the way these two are going.

I avoided naming these participants or identifying their sex, so no one could dismiss their story as that of a shrewish wife or an abusive husband—or vice versa! Either sex is capable of accusing and making problems worse than they merit.

Spouse A justifies his or her rampage by saying, "I'm feeling really angry, and I'm going to spill it, like they say to." This is an apparent reference to popular thinking of the day, which tends to advocate saying what you feel, getting your feelings out. There's a general attitude that bottled-up emotions produce cancer and heart attacks, and that releasing them is necessary to avoid tension and to promote deeper, more honest relationships.

Perhaps so. Proper release—in the right way, at the right time, to the right person—is helpful, and it can promote better relationships. However, when carried too far, this view is dangerous. What we've seen here is certainly not building relationships, and it seems to be creating its own tensions rather than releasing them.

While there are useful ways to reduce feelings of anger, most "ventilationists" point out that overly aggressive behavior becomes self-feeding and turns small anxieties into big ones. Which of us hasn't shouted at someone, only to find ourselves getting angrier the more we shouted? Who can doubt the "psych-up" value of the aggressive fist-jabbing movements many football players display after a successful tackle or quarterback sack. Emotions feed on themselves.

Look at the harmful and destructive language in the discussion above: "You didn't mean to keep your word." "Not another of your excuses." "You never do what you say." "It's like you try to make me upset." All of these are accusations against the other person rather than useful expressions of feelings.

Does a spouse have a right to express anger? Definitely. But how? How about this three-step process: First, delay. This is where one can simmer down, count to 10, 50, 100— whatever it takes to become calm. Second, decide. Will expressing these feelings improve or hurt the situation? In the short run? Long run?

Third, after analyzing questions like these, if this seems to be one of those times when expression is better than silence or delay, then by all means make an honest statement of feelings—but without blaming, accusing, or making the problem worse.

Compare Spouse A's approach with non-threatening statements like these: "I feel angry about the hoe and weeds in the yard. I think we need to talk. Now or later?"

Expressing anger is neither good nor bad in itself. It depends on the situation. Couples may feel free to express feelings, but only after thinking about the consequences, and after a commitment to civility, restraint, and empathy. None of these will give us cancer.

GROUND RULES

"OK, honey, I think we can talk now," Kelly said. "I got the baby settled down, and the other kids are finally getting to bed. What was on your mind?"

"Quick. Bar the door. Maybe we can get four minutes for ourselves," Lance said.

Kelly laughed, "Sometimes it is wild around here, isn't it? Did we know when we started out what having five kids would be like?"

Lance shook his head. "Are you kidding? Some things can't be understood without being there. And it's a good thing we didn't! But one thing I did know, Kelly Ann Webb Levine."

"Oh, and what's that, Lance William Levine?"

"That I loved you very much."

"My, aren't you romantic tonight."

"And still do."

"Keep talking. I'm all ears."

"And what I wanted to talk about will help us stay in love even more in the future," Lance said.

"I'm all for that, mister."

"OK, here's the deal. We've had our share of arguments over the years. Probably no more than normal. Sometimes we've managed to understand each other and come to a compromise or resolution. Other times, we haven't done so well. We've hurt each other, said things we shouldn't have, and maybe wounded the relationship." He paused. "Right?"

"Yes, and sometimes we've just dropped it because we couldn't agree."

"That's right. Well, I read an article a few months ago that's stuck with me. It talked about setting up ground rules for discussion, and it sounds like a good idea to me. You know, to take time, when there is no problem—like right now—to lay out a few guidelines for how to handle things when they do come up. Sort of a *Levines' Rules of Order,* I guess, so we stand a better chance of coming to solutions without hurting each other."

Kelly was thoughtful. "OK. Yes, it sounds good to me."

"You're hesitant," Lance said.

"Well, only because I'm not sure yet what you have in mind," Kelly said. "And, if I'm honest, I guess I still harbor the idea—romantic and idealistic as it is—that we ought to learn to control our tongues and love each other more and everything would be fine.

"Not that I believe that always works," Kelly went on. "When I really think about it, I know that things come up, people have feelings, biting the tongue isn't always best, and all that. But my first reaction is more the 'leave it alone and it will go away' idea.

"But never mind. I know certain things need to be talked out. Erase my hesitancy. I'm in favor."

"OK," Lance said. "Well, I listed here a few ideas—some I remember from the article, some are my own. These are only a beginning, and I'd want us to add to them. Maybe I can explain these, and you can think about them, then we'll talk about them tomorrow night.

"First, I wrote here, 'Listen, listen, listen.'—meaning to take the time to really understand the problem before wading in with the answer."

"OK," Kelly said.

"Next, 'Stop recycling.' "

"I think I know what that means," Kelly said. "We sometimes like to drag out all the old issues when we're in the middle of something."

"Exactly," Lance said. "It gets in the way, and takes us off the subject. Next, I have 'Set aside time.' What does that one mean to you?"

"You mean to bring things up when there's really time to discuss them, not necessarily right when they occur?" Kelly asked.

"That, plus making a regular time—once a week at least, maybe even daily, for a couple of minutes—to check in with each other and see how life in general is going, before things build up, you know?"

"I like that," Kelly said. "I think it would help a lot. We get so busy with the kids and everything, sometimes it's like we're strangers."

"Next . . ."

"Before you leave that one, Lance," Kelly said.

"Sure, what?"

"Well, I heard somewhere, at a church meeting, I think, a talk about that kind of daily meeting, and I remember that the woman speaking said she and her husband started out each session by talking only about the good things that had happened that day, and complimenting each other. This made them feel closer and kept them feeling good about each other. After that, they went into talking about specific categories as needed.

"They used a checklist with things like money, children, household chores—I remember those three."

Lance was writing them down. "Good. I'd add one right off, and that's talking about goals and plans. Sometimes I feel like we don't know what the other one intends, like a few years ago when you thought of our savings as for a piano—and thought I agreed—and all along I was thinking of a second car."

Lance and Kelly have a great list started, and a great idea: to set the ground rules for discussion while things are calm. With a little more work and some practice, they'll come up with enough basics that their arguments will be reduced, and those that occur will be better handled.

Couples can easily fall into the habit of really talking only when there's something to settle. How much better to talk regularly. Kelly's initial hesitancy is often typical. We've sometimes been raised to feel that disagreements are simply bad, and that if we were better people we wouldn't have them. We would simply exercise "Christian" restraint and let everything go by us.

It's a misguided idea. Christianity has nothing to do with it. Those people who allow no ripples ever to trouble the smooth surface of their marriage usually have a superficial marriage. They don't really relate, and they certainly don't grow as a couple. They merely co-exist, side by side, because they never know one another in depth. They avoid problems by avoiding real interaction with each other.

A realistic view tells us that two intelligent, distinct personalities are bound to view certain things differently, no matter how much alike they may be. Ground rules help provide a way to work through inevitable differences. And setting aside time for compliments and positive comments will ensure that at least some of the messages we send one another will be more than neutral or negative, but positive and uplifting.

Both spouses are responsible for improved communication in their marriage. Good communication is vital to the long-term as well as the day-to-day operation of a relationship.

QUESTIONS FOR DISCUSSION

Are we, as a couple, in the habit of talking? Do we agree on the amount of time to spend at it? Can we talk easily about small and large matters, or are we out of practice?

How do we talk? Are we mostly able to resolve problems and help one another without making the problem worse by making comments of the wrong type? How can we improve our ability not to "talk past" one another?

How are we at accepting new information and other points of view?

Are we effective listeners? Do we need to practice? Are we committed to the concept? Are we willing to stop a conversation when we're unclear and state our interest in understanding the other person's view?

How are we at holding our clever tongues? Do we hurt one another and cut each other off by smart remarks? How can we avoid this problem?

How are we at allowing varied emotions in each other over the same event?

Do we know how to express strong emotions without blaming each other or making the situation worse? Can we talk through how best to express these emotions? Would a few practice sessions help?

Do we both know the ground rules for discussion in our home? Do we have a regular time to positively share ideas and thoughts and to routinely discuss important matters?

CHAPTER 4

MORE
COMMUNICATION

Just when we think we've got the basics down—such as listening, stating our feelings, and seeing the other person's point of view—we discover additional parts of communication that are more subtle. Giving honest answers rather than expected ones, for instance, may be harder than it sounds. Looking behind the problem for the real problem, deciding whether to defend or to analyze an emotional response, trying to solve problems rather than merely to discuss them, showing an increase of love toward a spouse with whom we have had "words"—these and other "higher-level" communication skills are illustrated in this chapter.

Marriages improve when couples pay attention to the subtleties of communication. And not only marriages, but individuals, too. People make themselves better, not merely by their sensitivity to what they say and how they say it, but by their attention to what is behind their communication—what they find themselves thinking. For example, honesty compels us to recognize how we sometimes use speech to cover our thoughts and to make ourselves look better to others. As we look inward and uncover such motives, we become more open, integrated, and unthreatened — we become better individuals and better spouses.

One caution: No ideas about communication should be used to manipulate someone. Those who twist these ideas to get their own way, create guilt, or maintain control — rather than to improve understanding — sow distrust and deceit into the intimacy of marriage — the one institution that should be most free of such distortions.

EXPECTED ANSWERS

Nyla and Ward sat on their couch discussing one of their children who had carelessly lost her coat. Nyla had proposed letting her learn a lesson by not buying her a new one until the following year. Ward didn't like the idea. "Her friends would tease her that we can't afford a new coat," he said.

Nyla said, "Aren't you being a little too concerned about what people will think?"

"Of course not," Ward answered. "I just mentioned that; it's not my real motivation. But aren't you being overly harsh on certain of your children and consistently lenient with others?"

Nyla said, "Certainly not. How could you say that? I'm fair to all of them."

In this short exchange, each person asked a question that almost demanded a certain answer. We could be about as sure of the answer as if we had asked a Southerner whether the South really lost the Civil War. The structure of the question nearly guaranteed defensiveness. These expected answers quickly polarize discussion into two viewpoints, reducing the chance of agreement and getting in the way of honestly hearing what people really feel and why.

Don't parents make correct decisions for correct reasons? We all like to think so. Therefore, Ward would be unlikely to instantly agree that his decision might have been influenced by what outsiders would think. Also, since parents like to think they're fair to all their children, how could Nyla answer other than what she did?

And yet it's possible that Ward and Nyla observe in one another motives and characteristics that would bear discussing. Their assessments of each other may be pretty accurate. If so, wouldn't the discussion about their child's coat benefit from a closer look at the real motives?

Let's rerun this discussion, in two parts, for a closer look. First, we'll have Nyla gently probe Ward's thinking, rather than directly challenging him and drawing out an "expected" answer.

PART ONE

After Nyla made her proposal and heard Ward's response, she said, "What is it you don't like about sending Silvy to school with the coat she nearly outgrew last year? Through her own carelessness, she lost her new one, and I think she ought to accept the consequences."

"Well, it seems kind of cruel."

"The winter's nearly over, so the weather isn't that cold now."

"No, but the old coat is too tight, it's torn, and people will think we can't afford a new one."

That's when Nyla could say, "I guess I'm not too worried about what people say, if it teaches Silvy a lesson. Is that something you're worried about—what people will think?"

"Well, I guess it might be," Ward answered. "I don't want her classmates to ridicule her."

"Sometimes I'm anxious about how things will look, too. And I agree we should protect our kids from needless peer cruelty," Nyla said. "Let's talk about it."

PART TWO

When Nyla and Ward had finished talking about Ward's concern, he led into his thought about Nyla's treatment of her children. "Nyla, are you sure this isn't a pretty heavy punishment for an eight-year-old?"

"I don't think so," Nyla said. "Silvy has a major problem with remembering things. Why not help her learn?"

"I remember Jake losing his gloves last year. They turned up later, but what did we do in the meantime?"

"We bought him new ones, but gloves don't cost what coats do. And he didn't have the constant problem Silvy does."

"I just want to be sure we treat everyone fairly, and not be overly harsh on certain ones — or have them think we are. Can we talk about that?"

Ward and Nyla can now discuss their concerns without wading through accusations and judgments. Neither need feel defensive when concerns are handled properly.

Note that manipulation is not the purpose here. Both Nyla and Ward are talking in a way that will get honest responses and elicit discussion. They may not always agree, but their honest viewpoints will likely be revealed.

Without such approaches, a spouse feels attacked. Under attack, we generally respond with expected answers that get in the way of truth. If Ward's viewpoint needs to change, for example, he is more likely to be willing to change if he is brought to analyze and recognize his error himself than if Nyla throws it in his face. Then defensiveness takes over, and he defends what he might otherwise care little about.

When we present ideas gently, others are more likely to respond in honest ways that lead to agreements and changes of viewpoint, or, at least, deeper understanding of one another.

THE REAL PROBLEM

"I'm running out of things to say here, Walter. Do you want to add anything?" Sandy asked.

"Add anything to what?"

"This letter to my folks," Sandy said. "I want to mail it tomorrow."

Walter sat at the dining-room table across from his wife, papers and receipts spread before him. "Oh, I don't know. I've got to get these tax forms done. I can't think of anything to say, anyway."

"You ought to write a line once in a while, so they'd know you're still alive."

"And you wouldn't tell them if I wasn't?" Walter smiled. "Who'd do your taxes then? Well, what is it you want me to say?"

"Walter, if I have to tell you what to say, I'd just as well say it myself." Sandy sounded miffed. "I thought you might have something you wanted to say."

"Can't think of anything," Walter said shortly. "I'm not much of a letter-writer, you know."

"At least not to my folks."

"For crying out loud, Sandy. I'm not much of a letter-writer to anyone, not even my folks. Why are you trying to make something out of this?" Walter put down his pen. "I hardly write to any-

one, but because I don't have anything to say at
the moment to your folks, that's now a problem?"

"I thought you wrote your mom last week."

"I did," Walter exclaimed. "For the first time
in about three months!"

"So, I thought you might say a word to my
family, too."

"Oh, boy," Walter sighed. "Your folks don't
care what I say, anyway. Give me the letter. I'll
tell them all is well here in the Guinn household
today."

"Never mind," Sandy said as she stood up.
"Sorry I asked."

"Oh, walk away—a great way to solve a
problem," Walter said.

"Sorry I asked"—a sad way to end a conversation. But
this one seemed almost ended before it started. As any
observer could see, there's more going on here than a small
request by one spouse to write a few words and a simple
lack of anything to say by the other. This has to do with
a perception Sandy has of how Walter treats her family.
Note her "At least not to my folks."

It also has to do—according to Walter's statement
"Your folks don't care what I say, anyway"—with his perception of how he's viewed in Sandy's family.

Obviously, this is not a new topic to the Guinns.
Whether Walter and Sandy can clear up feelings that have
built up over the years depends on whether they will talk
about the real problem—their feelings and perceptions. If
they're not careful, they'll act like many politicians, wasting
time talking about the wrong things—such as whether
Sandy asks at inappropriate times or Walter is really too
busy today—and the problem will go unsolved. Even
worse, they may not talk about it at all. "Walking away"

may end the discussion, and Sandy could simply decide never to ask again. But the feelings will remain to pop up later in unexpected places.

Every person has misperceptions, and in every marriage are issues that could become problems because of these misperceptions. A topic that keeps coming up over several months or years, and always with the same negative result, is a candidate. Or if a topic doesn't ever come up—because one party or both have decided it's best avoided—this is another clue that the roots of the problem haven't been dug out.

It's risky to dissect a topic with heavy feelings attached. But finding the real problem is basic to meaningful discussion. It can be done if both parties decide to handle the matter in a loving, accepting way. If one spouse or the other can put aside his or her own feelings long enough to understand how the other is hurting, communication can take place.

TO DEFEND OR TO ANALYZE

"John, should we talk about last night?" Paula asked, as John dropped the last section of the morning paper on the carpet.

"Sure, I guess so," John answered.

"You want to start?"

"OK." He slid down from the couch onto the floor and leaned back. It was a favorite spot for him when he and his wife talked. "Well, I thought you shouldn't have kept the kids up so late—simple as that. Two of the three have coughs, and you're such a stickler for bedtimes when they're sick. I could hear them coughing more and more as it got to be 10:00, then 10:15, 10:30. I know you like Scrabble, but why you couldn't end the game, or set it aside until today, I couldn't understand. I mentioned quitting twice, saw that you didn't like it, and so gave up and went to bed.

"James was bugging Paige, and she'd lost interest long ago. She's too young for the game, anyway. She'd cried twice over minor things. I think she was just tired. I know it was a holiday, and you don't play often, but I still don't think it was worth it. I was in bed but noticed it was 11:15 before lights were out. That's it."

"OK. My turn? First, I want to apologize for snapping at you. I guess the second time you mentioned going to bed, I felt like you were pushing too hard. You're right that I don't get into these games very often, and I kept thinking we'd be done any minute. At 10:00 there were only five tiles left to choose from, after all. As for Paige, I told her twice to go to bed. But I suppose it's not realistic to expect her to want to leave the game, even though she was tired."

Paula paused, and John asked, "So what about your reaction? 'I'm an adult, too,' you said. What did that mean?"

"It seems strong now; it didn't then. I felt like you keep the kids up watching TV sometimes and now once a year I wanted to do something with them, and you didn't want me to."

After a few more exchanges for clarification, John said, "I expect that about handles the immediate problem. We got through that without much difficulty. But what I wonder is: Is there more behind it than that? Do you feel like you aren't treated as an equal partner—an adult— around here? To me, that's the key question. Shall we try to analyze that?"

Obviously, Paula and John have established a pattern of talking through their problems. And as things go, this one is probably not major. But they may gain much insight from their discussion, especially with their desire to analyze reactions and emotions and to seek the real problem behind the problem.

People often spend much energy defending why they feel certain ways. This after-the-fact explaining is suspect. It smacks of ego defense, of always wanting to be right. When we do this, we are reduced to acting like two-bit shysters, coming up with any justification for our actions.

How much better to analyze our reactions. It's possible, for example, that Paula's statement about being an adult too means a great deal. While the statement could mean, "Oh, letting the kids stay up late once won't hurt," it could also mean, "I want to be able to make more decisions in our home than I now feel I'm making." This would be a potentially serious message that, as a couple, John and Paula would need to recognize.

If we take the view that people's words often reveal more than they consciously intend, paying attention to the messages sent will help us look beyond defending—into analyzing. Most spouses are sometimes surprised to hear and feel themselves reacting to things they wouldn't have thought important. The next step is the critical one: whether to defend the strength of the reaction with newly thought-up reasons or to stop and look at the underlying feelings that might have caused the reaction, then to try to figure out what those feelings mean.

Of course, it isn't completely possible to analyze emotions. By definition they aren't easy to label and dissect. But if we accept the premise that every reaction has a cause, every emotion a source, then we have a better chance to find out what is really bothering us. We won't always be able to locate and define these sources, but it's the attitude of searching that's important.

PLAN AHEAD

Gene pulled into the driveway, turned off the car, and glanced at the digital clock on the dashboard: 5:47. Not too bad; he'd been later. At least it wasn't past dinner time, as it had been a few times lately. Getting away from a dental office right at the same time every day was tough.

"I hope dinner's ready on time tonight," he thought, but when he came through the kitchen door, he knew he would be disappointed again. The table wasn't set—in fact, it was covered with coloring books and crayons. The only evidence that dinner had even been considered was a pot simmering on the stove with little puffs of steam edging out from under the lid. Probably a vegetable, Gene thought. Meat, potatoes, salad—none of these were visible.

Just as Gene heaved a heavy sigh, his wife Tamara came into the room. The sigh cut off her greeting, and she said, "I know—late again. So are you. I was swamped."

"I didn't say . . . " he started, but he knew his sigh had betrayed him. And why not? Why shouldn't a man have a right to expect dinner on time, at least most evenings? He wasn't so callous that he didn't know there would be days when Tamara was overly busy. But dinner at six was mostly a matter of planning—he was convinced of that—and Tamara just didn't start on time. And here she was accusing him.

Gene said, " 'So are you,' you say. Well, I'm here as quick as I can be."

"And I'm getting dinner as quick as I can, too," Tamara said as she turned and opened the refrigerator. Gene went to the bedroom to change clothes.

Nobody is happy in this house tonight, and dinner is likely to be less than relaxing. It sounds as if Gene is late (or later than Tamara expects him) rather often. Also, dinner is frequently after the hour Gene expects it. Patterns have been established and feelings are at the blazing point.

However, patterns can be changed. Each partner can plan ahead—not only to start dinner or leave the office on time, but to better handle lapses.

Since Gene knows dinner is sometimes going to be late, why can't he consider—in advance—what to do when it is? A quick list might include taking a few bites of something to ease his hunger, helping Tamara get dinner finished and on the table, setting up a work program for the kids to help, or considering with his wife the possibility of moving the dinner hour to 6:15 or 6:30.

Likewise, since Tamara knows Gene is going to have trouble finishing his last appointment precisely at 5:00 every day, maybe she can adjust her thinking about his arrival time or ask him to have his receptionist call home when he's going to be late.

Most important, Gene and Tamara should include in their plans better internal responses like listening to one another's explanations when they are late and not letting sighs get in the way of greetings.

These are not surefire solutions, but they're a start toward better communication. Certainly, late arrivals or late dinners aren't the only conflict-producers; marriage has considerable potential for such irritations. But deciding in advance how to handle recurring problems can do much to lessen tensions and increase understanding.

PROBLEM-SOLVING

"Shireen," Doug said, "Sit down a minute, can you? We've talked about money before—usually by starting out blaming each other and ending up the same way. This time, I want to start by saying that I don't blame you for our budget shortfalls. But I'm worried. I foresee our having to take money out of savings again at the end of the year for property tax, Christmas, house insurance—one or all of the above. And that's scary to me."

"Me too," Shireen said. "It tells me we're not really living on our monthly income. We're exceeding it throughout the year."

"I'm afraid so. Yet when I look at our expenditures, nothing really seems out of line. I know we spend less on groceries than many families our size, and we drive older cars. We probably do spend more on summer trips than many of our neighbors do, but I think the trips are worth it. Of course, our house payments are high."

"How about things like utilities?" Shireen asked. "With the kids getting older, they take more, and longer, showers, and the downstairs furnace gets turned on more often than it used to."

"That needs to be looked at," Doug agreed. "We ought to get the family together and talk about it. But I think you and I need to look at the 'big picture' first. I mean, even if we cut down the heat bill by $5, $10, even $20 a month, that wouldn't make up for the $1,000 to $1,500 we're going to be short at the end of this year. Why don't we set a time when you and I can lay out the whole thing, without interruptions, and see what can be done to really look at the options."

Doug and Shireen stand a good chance of coming to grips with their money problem. Now that they've moved from their previous blaming and complaining to a willingness to solve their problems, their discussion will likely bear fruit. They may still be short of cash, of course—

talking about money seldom creates more of it—but they will more likely know why they are short. Then they can face the hard choices about how to spend less or earn more—the only two choices available.

Blaming wastes energy, hurts the relationship, and isn't likely to help people improve. Trying to solve problems, on the other hand, means that the spouses will gather information, look hard at causes, brainstorm solutions, and plan for change. It isn't always fun nor easy, but it's usually productive; it brings results rather than merely tired jaws.

Solving problems is as much a matter of attitude as of skill. Where both partners in a marriage decide to be part of the solution, communication will bring fine results.

TIMING

"What's this?" Les asked. He was helping get lunch on the table and had pulled a yogurt container from the fridge. "I don't know," Evie said. "I don't recognize it. Could be leftovers. I sometimes put them in those containers."

Les popped off the lid. "Whew!" he said. "I think it used to be yogurt. It's grown green fur."

"Ugh," Evie said. "Get rid of it. One of the kids must have started it and then forgot about it. Where in the world did you find it?"

"Oh, down on the bottom shelf, stashed in with all the other junk that's always back there."

Assuming Evie is primarily responsible for what's stored in the refrigerator, this last remark could be received as rather cutting, implying, as it does, Les's disgust at her sloppiness.

Since we're not privy to Les and Evie's fridge, we can't say whether, in fact, Evie is less than careful about what gets lost in there. But while we don't know Evie's habits, we can say something about Les: His timing is way off.

When a person habitually tosses cutting comments about his spouse into the middle of innocent conversations, he risks causing hurt feelings, resentment, and distrust of conversation with him in general. Communication isn't meant to resemble warfare; it shouldn't consist of sharp one-liners flung across the room.

A spouse with a pattern of such out-of-the-blue comments causes the other to be always on guard for the barbed arrows that can fly at any moment. And since constantly being on guard is tiring and not much fun, family members will come to avoid contact with the archer. Better no conversation than a dangerous one.

If Les is concerned about the way Evie stores food, he has a perfect right to speak with her about it—but at the right time, not when they are sitting down to lunch, which, depending on Evie's reaction to Les's attack, may now be tense indeed.

DON'T LOSE BY WINNING

Leon had it all worked out. He would have to present Roberta with his observations, though it would be painful for her. The last straw was when he'd come home from work today to find his two teenage boys not at home. Since Dee was grounded, he'd asked Roberta about it.

"I don't know where they are," Roberta said. "Suddenly, the car was gone and so were they."

When the boys came back about an hour later, Leon accused Dee of forgetting his grounding. Dee protested, "But Mom told me to go apply for a mall job she'd heard about."

Leon was frustrated. He went back to Roberta and told her what Dee had said.

"Dee says you sent him to the mall."

"Oh, that was an hour before," Roberta said. "He didn't go right away. I'd forgotten about it, and they didn't tell me where they were going when they left later."

Just because Dee didn't go when Roberta told him to, how could she forget she'd sent him and have no idea where he was? Leon couldn't figure it. Things like this had happened a lot recently. Leon could think of many times when Roberta seemed to remember things wrongly. One of the kids would come home later than expected and say, "I didn't say I'd be gone only an hour," to which Roberta would answer, "Oh, well, I guess I thought you did." But before the return, she had insisted to Leon that this was what was said.

Today's episode appeared to Leon a transparent way of keeping out of trouble with him, since he had implied negligence on Roberta's part in letting Dee go. She must have had some idea where the boys were, yet she gave Leon no clue. Her convenient lack of memory had caused Leon to unjustifiably attack his son.

Leon worried about an apparent pattern of telling only part of the story, and he decided to talk to Roberta about it. When he did, later that night, Roberta treated the matter as merely one of faulty memory.

"I just forgot," she said. "With so many kids telling me what they're doing and when, I don't always keep track, I guess. When the boys didn't go right away, by that time it had slipped my mind."

"But Roberta," Leon started . . .

What should Leon say at this point? He has a choice. He can accept Roberta's explanation, or he can tell her he sees her behavior as designed to keep herself "out of trouble" with him. He can present the other instances where that appeared to be the case. He can push his view and perhaps convince Roberta that her behavior appears dishonest or self-protective.

But he needs to weigh the costs. To accuse another adult—particularly a spouse—of dishonesty is to use a very big gun. It's a major step, one from which retreat may be impossible. One had better be sure the target warrants this much firepower.

Leon has already planted the idea that, in the case of Dee going to town, Roberta should have remembered what was going on. Now he would undoubtedly be better off to wait for further unimpeachable evidence of the same problem than to bring up nebulous past events without being able to recount the details. Otherwise, he may hurt his wife and their marriage a great deal.

Communication is more than merely exchanging information. It's also weighing and evaluating the expected results—and, at times, biting the tongue. Sometimes one can lose a great deal by winning.

SHOWING AN INCREASE OF LOVE

"Dear Kyle." Kyle had found the note and sat down on the bed to read it. "I know we had words this morning. I know, too, that we're both still upset, and the issue isn't settled yet. But I want to let you know that I love you very much, even when we disagree.

"Please know that I want to work this out so we both feel good about it, if possible. In the meantime, accept my love." The note was signed, "Marta."

At first, Kyle didn't know what to think. He'd never argued with anyone who wrote a love note in the middle of the fight. He wondered if it was meant as a kind of one-upmanship. Be he knew his wife wasn't that way. She

said what she meant and meant what she said;
she wouldn't use words to make herself look better in some way.

Kyle read the note again and saw clearly
there was nothing in it designed to put him
down; it was just what it seemed to be—a love
note, a statement of commitment to the relationship—in spite of present difficulties. With that
conclusion, Kyle decided this was the way it
should be: honest, sometimes painful, discussion
was acceptable—even in a new marriage—as long
as it was clear that love still reigned.

Kyle felt a surge of love for his young wife.
He found it difficult to tell her so, at times, especially when he was upset that she couldn't see
certain matters the way he did. He knew it
would be hard right now, but he would tell her
of his love anyway. Then, whenever they might
actually finish this particular debate—as they'd
agreed to do "later"—they would remain friends,
not enemies, and the underpinnings of their marriage would not be threatened.

"First fights" inevitably occur. Two strong, intelligent
people are bound to have differing views on many things,
and sooner or later, some of these differences are going to
matter enough to one or both that "words" will ensue.

Perhaps neither party will be persuaded to change his
or her view on the matter. Fifty years may pass without
agreement on certain issues. What matters is what Kyle
calls the "underpinnings" of the relationship. A couple
can agree to disagree on things as diverse as politics, child-
rearing, careers, and budgeting. But none of these—as
troublesome as each of them can be at times—need
threaten a marriage. If people can learn to use good problem-solving techniques, can compromise, can see the other

point of view, and can give in on occasion, their love will endure.

However, one must never assume that a spouse is always certain of that love. In moments of stress, a partner may need reassurance. When love is needed most, it's sometimes the hardest to express, but it must be done. Especially following a disagreement.

When times are the toughest, couples must remember the love that holds them together, and express it to one another. Not condescendingly as in "You're wrong, but I love you anyway," nor to win points in the discussion — but just to make sure the foundation holds in the storm. This is communication in its purest, most loving form.

QUESTIONS FOR DISCUSSION

How are we at presenting things in non-accusing ways, so that "expected" answers are reduced and honest discussion increased?

Are there problems that keep coming up at our house in one form or another that we haven't ever sought the basis for? Could we choose one or two to talk about in an effort, not to blame, but to look for real causes?

How are we at looking behind our emotional reactions at their bases — analyzing rather than defending? Do we encourage such analysis and work to understand one another?

How are we at planning ahead to better handle problems that may arise? Are there specific things in our lives right now that could benefit from such an approach?

How are we at solving problems as a couple? Are there problems now bothering us that could benefit from a decision to find solutions rather than simply to complain?

How is our communication timing?

How are we at avoiding pushing things so far that we lose by winning and hurt more than necessary? Do we leave room for a person to change on his or her own?

What are some of the times when an expression of love meant the most to each of us? How are we at reassuring one another of our love, especially during difficult times? Are there ways of showing love that mean more than saying?

CHAPTER 5

RESPONSIBILITY FOR THE RELATIONSHIP

One of the distinguishing traits of serious dating or courtship is the vigor the participants usually give the relationship. Serious young daters may, indeed, spend the bulk of their time, money, and energy on one another.

Both find their beloved the most fascinating subject on earth. They want to know all about how he or she thinks and sees things. Often, they're willing to change themselves into better people to please their partner. When problems develop or they sense difficulties, they expend great effort to improve the situation. Each party seems willing to take responsibility for making the relationship as perfect as possible.

Alas, a relationship probably cannot continue with such force throughout a lifetime. Other demands reduce the time and energy once given; certain other things simply must be accomplished in life, and these detract from the energy available for the relationship. Because of competing demands, many couples find their union stagnating.

Yet, while "settling down" to a more comfortable, less frenetic courting schedule is expected and required, each spouse must continue to consider that he or she is responsible for the relationship and its growth, rather than leaving that responsibility to the other spouse or to chance.

When both parties decide to cultivate their relationship, their marriage will succeed. The messages they send each other will clearly convey their mutual interest in the relationship. Because of this, they can't fail.

In this chapter, several couples look at issues designed to help ensure a growing relationship.

MAKE MARRIAGE A PRIORITY

"I knew your advanced age would catch up with you soon, boy. This is twice in a row I've beat you."

"Hey, JD, turning forty had nothing to do with it. I'm still the handball champ of this extended family. Beating you three times a week for the last eight years got a little boring, that's all. I decided a guy ought to build up his kid brother's confidence once in a while. Wait till Friday."

JD laughed. "Sure, sure, whatever you say, big brother. Big, older brother."

"Hurry up, there, young 'un," Al said. "I've got to get back to a meeting."

"I'm about ready."

"That's one thing I can still beat you at," Al grinned. "From the time you were a kid, you always were a slow dresser."

Al closed his locker and stood waiting, one foot up on the bench, while JD finished buttoning his shirt. The two brothers were employed in buildings a few blocks apart and enjoyed meeting in a city recreation center three times a week for handball at lunch hour.

"Speaking of Friday," JD said, "you're going to be out of town, aren't you? On that midwest fund-raiser?"

"Nope. I moved that to next Wednesday and Thursday."

"Oh, OK. Want to run, then, as usual?"

"Nope. No more running on Friday nights," Al said.

"Looks like turning forty has slowed you down in quite a few ways."

"Says you, JD. Fact is, I can't run for the same reason I moved the trip. Pam and I've decided to make Friday a regular date night."

JD looked at his brother. "Well, that's a good idea. Tina and I have tried it, too, off and on. You must be pretty serious, though, if you're rescheduling trips and all."

"We are," Al said. "Oh, we know there'll be times when we can't manage—I travel too much to move all my trips. But while the idea is still new, I wanted to be sure and get started right and not sabotage the plan right off."

"Well, good luck. I don't see how you're going to manage, though," JD said, as he closed his locker door and picked up his duffel bag. "As busy as we are, Tina and I are just hit and miss at our dates."

"Well, here's how I came to the decision that it could be done. I'll ask you the same question I asked myself: how many hours do you spend on physical fitness in a week?"

"Oh, the same as you. Handball three lunch hours a week, plus running two evenings. About five hours, I guess."

"Right," Al said, "And that doesn't count getting ready and getting cleaned up afterward. More like eight or nine hours a week, I figured. Then I thought: how many hours do I spend on

building up my marriage? Well, the answer
didn't compare very well."

As Al has discovered, spending time as a couple takes
planning and commitment. There's lots of competition for
our time, and it seems like they don't make days as long
as they used to. Even the family takes time away from the
couple, but marriage partners need to reserve a certain
amount of time for themselves.

For a couple with a growing family demanding and
deserving attention, creating the opportunities for time
together won't be simple. The setting of a firm, predeter-
mined hour, as Al and Pam have done, is a necessary step
for most couples. Otherwise, the time simply won't be
there. We'll never find more time; we can only decide how
best to use what we have.

An attitude that makes the spouse an important and
necessary part of the day is vital. How this is done can
vary from couple to couple, but however each couple decides to make it so, the marriage must become a priority.
It is the central family relationship, and if the center doesn't
hold, all is lost.

TALK ABOUT THE RELATIONSHIP

"I don't know if we want to talk about all of
these tonight, but there are some good ideas
here," Nick said.

"I'm glad you agree," Lila said. "I thought
so, too, when I saw the list in a book the other
day. I wanted to see what you thought. I really
think it could help us in our marriage. Not that
we're having big problems, but I think any
couple needs to keep their relationship growing."

Nick was still scanning down the list. "Look
at this one: 'What are three strengths a family
counselor would see if he were to look in on our
marriage? Three weaknesses?'

"Could be interesting," Nick went on. "And here: 'What are several key words to describe our marriage? To describe each of us as individuals? As parents?' These could be tough."

Lila said, "Yes, but I like the idea behind it— couples shouldn't get together to talk about just problems and concerns. They also need to talk about the relationship itself, how it's changing, what stresses each person is feeling, how they would like to see things improve. It's the positive approach I like."

"Me, too, but some of these could be a little threatening, couldn't they? I mean, to have to list your best and worst traits and those of your spouse, as they affect the marriage?"

"Well, we can skip any part we want, or change the list, or whatever. It's just a guideline. And, of course, a willingness to be open about things is vital. I think we could handle it. Don't you?"

"It's worth a try."

Lila and Nick have started a process that will undoubtedly produce good results for their marriage. When a couple decides to talk about their relationship as something to which they're both committed and which they both want to improve, the stage is set for growth.

A list of questions like Lila's is a good starting point for a couple to discuss their relationship:

1. What are three strengths a family counselor would see if he were to look in on our marriage? What are three weaknesses?

2. What are several key words I would use to describe our marriage? To describe each of us as individuals? As parents?

3. Individually, what are my greatest needs in our marriage? What do I want most from the marriage?

4. What are the main stress points in our marriage?

5. Identify the changes occurring in our marriage. What has been the effect of these changes?

6. What do I hurt about?

7. What am I happy about?

8. What do I believe my spouse wants?

9. What are my best traits, styles, approaches?

10. What are my worst traits, styles, approaches?

11. What are my spouse's best traits, styles, approaches, from my viewpoint?

12. What are my spouse's worst traits, styles, approaches, from my viewpoint?

13. To what degree does each good and bad trait, style, or approach help or hurt our relationship?

14. What improvements would each of us make in ourselves?

A couple with courage and the proper attitude can learn a lot from such a discussion list, especially if they will follow certain guidelines:

— Be specific.

— Be honest, but not brutal or blaming.

— Say, "I feel . . . ," "I like it when . . . ," or "I would like . . . ," rather than "You always . . . " or "You never. . . . "

— Expect to have differing views.

— Listen.

— Don't force answers. Either spouse may choose to skip any item. Be sensitive to items that are too intense.

— Don't argue.

— Look for solutions, but don't expect to become perfectly compatible in very many categories right away.

— Plan to talk regularly about differences, and continue to go over the list occasionally for new items and new feelings.

With guidelines like these, a couple can understand each other better and can improve the basis of their marriage. A marriage relationship is more than just the sum of two individuals. It has a life of its own, and it needs care like any other living thing. And it isn't a cactus, needing nourishment only occasionally. It's a tender vine that needs constant attention. The key is that both parties are responsible for that care.

COMMITMENT

"So this is the young man I've been hearing about," Arlo Lamson said as he extended his hand. He'd already hugged his granddaughter LeeAnn, and he now shook hands with her fiancé.

"I'm glad to meet you, Mr. Lamson," Blair said.

"Just as well call me Arlo, or Grandpa, like LeeAnn and everybody else does. Come in and sit down. I'm awful glad you two could come by."

"Wouldn't have missed seeing you, Grandpa," LeeAnn said. "I don't bring home future husbands every day to meet my folks. And you're part of the deal, too."

"Well, I might scare him right out of the decision, you know. But I'm sure glad you'd come by, LeeAnn. You always were my favorite, you know."

"Oh, I know," LeeAnn laughed. "Along with Lois, Tucker, Aaron, Alysa, and all the rest. Whoever's here at the moment, right?"

"And what's wrong with that?"

"He only has about twenty grandkids . . . " LeeAnn said to Blair.

"Twenty-two and a half," Arlo interrupted.

" . . . and from the time we could talk, he's always told each of us that we're his favorite."

"And it's true. Absolutely. It's like ice cream. When I'm eating chocolate, chocolate's my favorite. If I have a bowl of strawberry in front of me, that's my favorite. Makes sense, doesn't it, Blair?"

"Yes, sir, whatever you say," Blair grinned.

"Oh, say, LeeAnn, this lad will do well in this family. Sounds like he's quite trainable," Arlo said, and they all laughed.

After a moment, Arlo said, "Wish your grandma could've met him."

"Me, too," LeeAnn said. "It's been a year this month, hasn't it."

"Fifty-four years we had, LeeAnn. If you two can do that well, you'll be fine."

The room was silent for a moment, then Blair asked, "How do we do it, Mr. . . . uh, Grandpa Lamson? What's the secret?"

"Well," Arlo answered, "Now you've come to the right place. Nobody loves to give advice like I do. In fact, if you hadn't asked, I'd have told you anyway."

LeeAnn and Blair gave one another amused smiles.

"I've thought over that question many times," Arlo began. "Why we stayed together and so many others didn't. Of course, more people did stay together in our day. None of my eight brothers and sisters ever got a divorce. Some were widowed early and remarried, but there was not one divorce.

"When it comes down to the next generation—your dad and mom's, LeeAnn—well, the nine of us had twenty-eight kids that lived to marry. Last count, there were six divorces. Thank heavens your folks aren't in that group.

"Now, that's bad enough, but what about your generation? I read the other day some horribly high figure I can't remember about the number of people who get married these days and their chances of divorce. Now I know there are lots of changes in the way people think since I was growing up. And I'm not such a fogey that I reject all of those—I think a lot of them are great. But something has sure slipped in the area of commitment."

Arlo scratched his head in puzzlement. "My neighbor here told me the other day that her granddaughter is getting married and had told her grandma, 'If it doesn't work out, we'll just have to get a divorce. Not that I want that,' she said, 'but you have to be realistic.'

"Well, my word, when you start out with that kind of idea, it's no wonder. Realistic! In our day, old-fashioned as it may seem, divorce was simply not an option. Martha and I had our problems—I needed a lot of taming—but we were committed. We may not have known much about what they now call enrichment and feedback and support and such, but we sure didn't carry in the back of our minds, 'Well, if it doesn't work out, we'll just get a divorce.' "

Commitment. What great thing was ever accomplished without it? A couple who starts out with the idea of possible failure has programmed their minds, at least in part, to fail. Of course, we all know that divorce is a legal option, technically available to any couple. But if we see it as a real option, we will hurt our chances.

It's like a man driving a car along a mountain road with a 500-foot drop-off. Defensive driving tells him to be alert to "escape routes," places he can turn to avoid problems.

Technically, he's aware that turning over the drop-off is one of his options. But surely he doesn't consider it a real one. It's an escape route all right—but only from one danger into what may prove to be a much greater one.

One of the myths of marriage is that divorce and a new start will wipe the slate clean and allow people to start again. Yet those who have gone through divorce—even when it was necessary to get away from abuse or some other major problem—often describe it as exchanging one set of problems for another. Census Bureau statistics also indicate a slightly greater likelihood of divorce in the second marriage than in the first. And studies show that five years into the second marriage, most couples are still struggling with adjustments; the transition was not so smooth after all. It appears that new starts are pretty tough to manage.

Lots of things have changed in the world, but Grandpa Lamson's view of marriage is still the only tenable one: commitment rather than escape routes.

LOYALTY

Penny leaned closer to be heard over the noise of the party. "I don't know, June," she said. "I'd only tell you, of course, but Glayd and I just aren't doing too well lately."

"Oh, really?" June asked.

"Yeah, it's tough. I mean, we've been married nearly three years, but in some things he's so stubborn, you know? I guess I could be part of the problem, but I feel like I do my best. When I try to get him to help me around the house, for example—I mean, I work, too, you know, so I feel like we ought to share the housework—when I can't take it any longer and yell at him to help, he just sits there and totally ignores me. It's really frustrating."

June shook her head and made a little click with her tongue.

"Really, the man is basically lazy, you know?" Penny concluded.

Across the room, Penny's husband, Glayd, was carrying on a conversation of his own. "Hey, Lynnette," he said, "great cake."

"Thanks, Glayd," Lynnette said.

Glayd raised his voice, as if he wanted Penny to hear him. "I wish I had a cook around my house like you, Lynnette. The last time my cook tried to bake a cake, the cake-mix box caught fire in the oven." He laughed loudly at his little joke. But there was no evidence Penny heard, since she was still talking in a conspiratorial tone to June.

"I hope Ross appreciates what he's got here, Lynnette," Glayd said, winking. "Somebody just might steal you away."

Obviously, these two episodes are meant as negative examples of loyalty to the marriage relationship. Penny is confiding details of her concerns about her husband that June has no business hearing. She's also labeling and undercutting him as a person. Penny would defend her actions by saying that June is an old friend, and that a woman has to talk to someone who understands. Uh-huh, sure thing.

Glayd is equally guilty of disloyalty. Though he would say his motive is mere fun, he is making Penny the brunt of a public joke. His other actions constitute flirting with Lynnette — even if mock flirting, for the purpose of attracting Penny's attention — certainly a no-no for a married man.

Both Penny and Glayd would probably argue that they are loyal to the institution of marriage. They might be shocked for us to suggest that they are not. Neither of them has technically broken any marriage vows; after all, they're only guilty of talk. However, while they may be converted to the principle of marriage, they are anything but loyal to each other.

A loyal spouse confides in no one outside the marriage about relationship problems or negative personality traits. (The only exception is when serious problems exist and professional help is sought.) A loyal spouse does not make his or her partner the brunt of public jokes. A loyal spouse doesn't give any kind of "come-on" signals to another— whether with serious intent or not.

Loyalty to the marriage and to one another is absolutely necessary for couples who accept responsibility for the marriage relationship.

WILLINGNESS TO GIVE

"Elaine," Todd sighed, "I really don't think I'm that bad a husband. I help quite a lot with the baby, but I do work all day, you know. I feel like saying 'I gave at the office.' "

"Great," Elaine said, tossing the dishcloth into the sink. "You go to work all day, so you feel you can come home and relax. What about me? Don't you think I 'work' all day, too? Just because I stay home to do my work, does that mean I don't need a break?"

"I know you work, Elaine. But I just see taking care of the baby as more your responsibility than mine. You wanted a baby—so did I—but you're the mother, and I guess I'm surprised you don't want to handle the main work involved."

"I am willing to handle the main work," Elaine retorted. "But I feel like I do 99 percent of it! You change maybe three diapers a week, you never feed him, and I always get up in the night."

"Elaine, you don't have to get up and go to work—I mean out to work. I can't get behind in my sleep and still do a good job—"

"OK. I don't know the answer, Todd," Elaine said. "I feel like I need . . . I guess it's not that I need help with the baby as much as I need a break, a change, a chance to do something else. When you come home and spend time in your shop on your woodworking, and I've had nothing but baby, baby, baby all day and had hoped for a little time with you, or something, I don't know. . . . I don't want you to give up your hobbies, but . . . "

"It sure sounds like it. I do my fair share in this marriage, that's all. When you add in my work at the office, I think I do at least my 50 percent."

"My 50 percent," Todd calls it—his "fair share." Well, technically, that's what each party ought to do, I suppose. Two able-bodied people each doing 50 percent should manage rather well. Like two draft horses each pulling half the weight, they would theoretically pull the load. Yet we hear from numerous sources that each marriage partner ought to give 100 percent or 110 percent or some such figure. Mathematically, of course, 110 percent is impossible. But math has little to do with a good marriage. Attitude does. When both spouses have the attitude that they will give more than their required share, the relationship will grow, because each will find ways to contribute.

Todd and Elaine both may have unrealistic expectations; these often get worked out with the passage of time. What they will learn is how each of them can best contribute to the relationship. Todd may find he's able to take full charge of the baby for a certain time regularly, even if both agree that the main task is still Elaine's. Elaine may learn to develop interests she can carry on at home during this period of her life, while still caring more or less full time for a baby.

Certainly each marriage partner needs to do his or her "fair share." But in a successful relationship, where both spouses feel responsible for growth, each will need to view that share as a lot more than 50 percent. Unlike draft horses, marriage partners are doing a great deal more than merely pulling a load. They're not only getting a job done— they're building a relationship.

WHAT WILL YOU GIVE UP?

At the sound of the first bell, Sister Rogers hurried to summarize her lesson. "This has been a good discussion, I think. Now, I'd like to leave you with one final thought today. As young adults, you are preparing yourselves in many ways for marriage. You're maturing, learning about yourselves and others, and becoming more aware of what kind of person you want in a partner.

"We tend to think that when we meet the right person, he or she will make us happy, will give us what we need to be fulfilled. And we expect reciprocation—that the right person will find in us what he or she needs to be happy.

"And this is exactly what happens, to an extent. But what isn't so clear, I think, at your age, is that anything good requires a sacrifice. When you fall in love with someone, you're willing to give a great deal to this other special person. My question for you to think about is: What are you willing to give up? Not only give, but give up."

The class was attentive, but no recognition showed on any faces yet. Sister Rogers went on. "Let's name an easy one first. How about privacy? How much time do you spend alone every day and how important is that time to you?

"Here's a harder one to pin down: How about something like sarcasm? Are you willing to give that up to avoid extra strain on the relationship, even when sarcasm and cutting remarks might be your preferred, established style?

"Or what if you had to give up your need to 'win' every argument? Some people seem to actually start them, you know, just to keep in practice at winning."

Several smiled at the idea, and Sister Rogers went on, "We're going fast, I know, because we're nearly out of time, but do you see what I'm saying? All of us possess traits that will contribute wonderful things to a marriage, and we also possess other traits that will not help, and might hurt, it. You won't know you have some of these until you actually get into the marriage. Others, I'll bet you could identify right now. It's a pretty safe bet that the things that bug your roommates or your parents will also be a problem to your spouse."

As the second bell rang, Sister Rogers concluded, "Think about it, and see if you can identify some things you may need to give up. Then start working on a few so your poor spouse won't have to suffer through all of them with you. Thanks, and see you next week."

What are we willing to give up for the marriage relationship? In big and little ways, successful couples adjust— which sometimes means giving up part of themselves. In marriage, there are numerous matters requiring us to change certain viewpoints or behaviors as we learn to work with another person. Careers may be altered or abandoned entirely, the number and spacing of children may have to be negotiated, where we live—how close to relatives, how far from relatives—what we do for recreation and with whom, etc., etc., etc. All these are matters each of us has views on, and our partner will likely have different views on many of them.

In personal behavior, we often have to give up traits we've come to love: laziness, sloppy thinking, pride, negativism—the choicest of the rotten stuff. The willingness of two people to bend for the relationship determines, in large part, the success of the marriage. Some things may be hard to give up, but if we're committed to the marriage, we'll be willing to sacrifice for its growth.

As the Sunday School class of young adults rose to go, a few came up to thank Sister Rogers for her lesson. "It really made me think," said one.

A young woman lingered a moment until the others had left, and said, "Sister Rogers."

"Yes, Gina."

"That was an interesting lesson. It made me think of a lady in the ward I moved from. She was married and had three little kids. They were active in the church and everything; then, one day, she just left. Just went away, and they didn't even know where she was for a few days. Then she called and said she'd gone to another town and needed to do 'things on her own,' or something, and she wouldn't be back." Gina shook her head. "It really blew everybody away, you know. It was sad."

Sister Rogers nodded. "It must have been."

"Well, in light of your lesson," Gina said, "I guess she wasn't willing to give or give up, or something."

"You may be right. Something like that is

devastating to the family, and it's very unusual behavior, that's for sure. On the other hand, I think some people feel they've given or given up too much. They start to feel like their life isn't their own, like they've done nothing but conform, their whole life long, and now it's time for themselves for once.

"We can't judge such a thing, but I do believe it's possible to give up too much, to be raised in a way that the self has no chance to develop. Then all of our giving or conforming or going along is hollow—like pouring from an empty pitcher. We look at these cases and say this person wasn't willing to give—but maybe she simply gave too much for too long, and in the wrong way."

Jesus said, "He that loseth his life shall find it." How is it possible, then, to give too much? Well, one can only give from a reservoir of strength. It appears to be a human need to think for ourselves and to make decisions, to use our agency in big and little choices throughout our lives. When people become programmed to total conformity and to having no views of their own, they've given too much, in the wrong way, and that can be dangerous. They are a frantic series of choices just waiting to happen.

One who loses one's self by choice, by intelligent selection among options, differs significantly from one who feels continually forced, through mindless conformity, to do what everyone else wants. This kind of "giving up" is negative rather than positive.

GOALS AND PLANS

"What if they make me an offer I can't refuse?" Bryan asked quietly. Though she was in the seat right beside him, Nadine could hardly hear Bryan's voice over the sound of the jet engines.

She asked, "Isn't that what you want?"

"I guess so."

"You're letting them fly us to the interview, so I guess you're prepared for whatever comes," Nadine said. "Although we don't have to tell them right away, do we?"

"No, they'd let us have some time."

Nadine looked out the window at the cloud layer far below them. After several minutes, she asked, "Do you want to make this move?"

"Well, now that we're on the plane to the interview, I don't really know. I suppose I want to have the chance at it. After that, I don't know."

"You know," Nadine said, "I think we need to do some thinking and talking about our goals and plans for the future. Two of the kids are close to being on their own now; our family at home will be smaller in the next few years. And it's been a long time since we did any organized looking at where we want to be in the next decade."

"That's right," Bryan agreed. "We did that several times years ago, and we'd better do it again. We can wait until we see whether we get this job offer before we finalize anything, but let's spend time before we land mapping out a few 'what if's,' shall we?"

Nadine and Bryan are at one of life's crossroads. Even if they don't accept the new job or if the offer doesn't come, they can still work out which path they want to take, how they'd like things to be. A couple needn't always take what life offers; they can have a great deal to say about it.

Many people feel tied down because of job or children,

fearing that a major change would hurt their family. Others have made successful mid-career moves and have credited that decision with great benefit for themselves, their marriage, and their families. Change isn't good or bad in itself; our attitude toward it makes the difference.

All of us are on a jet plane headed somewhere. While destinations aren't completely clear, couples who discuss their goals will know better where they really are when they land as well as where they want to fly next.

SHARED HISTORY

"Our next speaker will be Brother Solen's youngest daughter, Marjean, who would like to make a few remarks."

Marjean got up from the front row where the rest of the family sat and came forward to the podium.

"Thank you, Bishop. I'm not on the program, but I asked if I could say something about my dad. I realize that most of you, members of his ward here, didn't really know Dad as we knew him growing up. Though he moved here to the condominium eight years ago, and though he was healthy and busy and involved with you nearly up to the end, the Parker Solen you knew was the Parker Solen without Mary Solen. Most of you probably know that Mom died in California the year before Dad moved here."

Marjean looked down at the dark, polished wood of the casket before her. "The others on the program have done a wonderful job of portraying Dad's life, but there's one element I wanted to reinforce. Maybe it's more clear to me because I was the youngest child and watched my parents grow old together before I left home. The thing I observed was how much unity my

parents had, how much of their history was
shared. I'll try to explain what I mean.

"When I read the obituary in the paper the
other night, I realized that little write-up just
couldn't say very much. Though I helped com-
pose it, it was bare compared to how Dad's life
really was."

Marjean moved the microphone up an inch
and back down an inch, an unconscious gesture
of nervousness. "The paper said, for example,
that Dad started his business forty-one years ago.
What it didn't say is how he and Mom talked
and labored and struggled to prepare to take that
big step, and how they worked hard at it for the
next several decades. All of this is in Mom's journal I've been looking through the last few days;
Dad didn't keep one.

"Now, I don't mean this to be one of those
'behind-every-great-man' speeches that somehow
come across as demeaning to women, although
they're intended as compliments. In my parents'
case, they were definitely behind each other, but
that's not the point. I'm not talking about support of one another as much as I'm talking about
a sharing, a blending, a history as a couple."

Marjean wiped her eyes once and went on. "I
noticed this in everything, even the way Mom
and Dad talked about the past. It was always
'we' and 'us,' not 'I' or 'me.' We were called
'our' kids, never 'my' kids. I noticed that, without realizing it, Dad, in recent years, said 'we'
even when he was talking about things that happened before he met Mom.

"I think this was one of the most beautiful
things about my parents. They really established
a unity, a oneness. They consciously worked at

it, and together they were more than one plus one; they created a new entity as a couple."

Marjean has pointed out an ideal for any couple to strive for—a unity, a shared history. People vary in the degree to which they unite and create a new identity. Some couples never really feel part of one another. Others, while still retaining individuality, combine to make a newness, a combination, a blend, a new recipe never before baked.

Successful couples relish in a shared history, whether in difficulties or in joys. They've gone through certain unique things together, things no other couple has experienced in just the same ways, and their relationship is strengthened because of it.

Couples of any age can purposely strive to create such a history, and to communicate its strength to their children.

WHO'S RESPONSIBLE FOR ME?

"I'd have never let you drag me into this conversation," Norman said angrily, "if I'd known you were going to blame me for everything that's ever happened to you. You always make me feel responsible, and leave me mad and upset."

"A typical statement from you, Norman," Ellen said. "You never want to do anything I want to do. If I want to talk, you don't."

"Why should I want to do something that upsets me?"

"So you would understand my concern, maybe," Ellen retorted. "Which, as I was saying, is that you never do anything to try to make me happy. You go to work, come home, watch TV, fall into bed, get up, and start all over again. I suggest going places, but you're not interested."

"I ought to go someplace, all right, to get away from your nagging."

Norman and Ellen have a problem, perhaps a major one. They blame each other for their lack of happiness. Notice Norman's statement: "You always make me feel responsible, and leave me mad and upset." Likewise, Ellen's: "You never do anything to try to make me happy."

Now, wait a minute. These folks are all mixed up. Must George feel the way he says Ellen "makes" him feel? And does Ellen have a right to expect George to make her happy? These are major questions in any marriage. And while this chapter has dealt with the matter of each partner taking responsibility for the relationship, that's quite different from taking responsibility for the happiness of another person. That's a burden we must never shoulder.

There is only one person responsible for my happiness—me. I recognize that certain others could help and that outside events could contribute, but I must never forget who ultimately decides how I will feel—me. I can ask for help and explore my needs with my spouse, yet I must accept the basic and inescapable responsibility for my own progress, success, and happiness in life. If I have a problem with this, then I know where I must begin; paraphrasing Pogo, I have to recognize that I have met the enemy, and he is me.

QUESTIONS FOR DISCUSSION

Is our relationship a priority? What can be done to enhance its position in relation to other important responsibilities?

Do we need to talk about our relationship and its growth more regularly?

How do we rate our commitment to working things through, no matter how difficult?

How do we rate our loyalty to our relationship? Our loyalty to one another individually?

How willing are we to give to the relationship more than is necessarily a "fair share"?

Are we willing to give up obstacles to improved relationships?

Do we agree on our goals for the next month, year, decade? Do we need to be more specific about our goals?

How do we feel about our shared history? How can we emphasize and relish the unique experiences we've had as a couple?

How are we at accepting responsibility for our own happiness as individuals, rather than blaming others?

CHAPTER 6

CONTROLS

The best marriages are partnerships. Manipulation and controls have no place in them. Rather, the partners in such relationships show acceptance and equality.

Other marriages suffer from a lack of equality and balance. Even the partners' everyday language indicates that one spouse claims ownership and the right to control the other. It is an extremely negative message.

People also live under controls they have placed on themselves or have had placed on them by their upbringing, often without their recognition. These limit or direct how they respond to certain situations. Together, these inner controls and the controls people sometimes place on each other greatly affect the marriage relationship.

When we insist on controlling the agenda, demand certain reactions, or expect every activity to be shared by both spouses, we exert unwarranted control over our mate. Controls are not necessary or proper in marriage, which should be a relationship of equals. But freeing ourselves from controlling behavior is sometimes difficult. Recognition is the first, and often the hardest, step.

In the following examples, couples struggle with a few of these difficult issues of freedom and control.

CONTROLLING THE AGENDA

The time is 7:45 A.M. at the Huff household. Leslie is unhappily seated at the piano bench.

"I don't have time this morning, Mom," she says. "I'll practice after school."

"That's what you always say, but you seem to forget."

"I won't today."

Leslie continues to play halfheartedly for a few moments. Finally she says, "Mom, I need to leave at 8:10. I told you last night. I won't have time to—"

Her mother snaps, "Do we have to argue about it during your practice time?"

Ted, finishing his breakfast, looks at his wife. He says nothing, but he thinks, "When else can she talk about it? You're making her practice; she's telling you she has to leave, and you won't let her talk about it."

It's now 7:55. Ted has now brushed his teeth and has his coat on. Leslie still plunks on the keys, tears running down her face. He kisses the top of her head and says, "Bye-bye, honey." Leslie says nothing. As Ted kisses his wife, he says—very quietly, so as not to create a scene or indicate disunity before his daughter—"A lot of pressure."

Phyllis answers, in a loud voice, "I could use some support." Ted goes out the door.

Here is a case where the agenda is controlled entirely by Phyllis. She insists on morning practice time, disallowing any discussion from her daughter, although minutes are passing and there will be no other opportunity for Leslie to make the point that she has to leave. Ted isn't allowed an opinion, either, even when he states it quietly. Phyllis simply won't hear the opinions of others, not this morning, at least. If Phyllis were a judge, she would be gaveling for silence or clearing the courtroom.

Spouses sometimes control one another and others by controlling the agenda. They won't talk unless it's their idea. They won't listen except when they choose to.

Some spouses control the agenda by skillfully maneuvering a conversation so that points others may wish to make are diverted. Rather than listening to what is being said, they say things like, "Oh, I thought you were going to say . . ." or "That reminds me . . ." or "Not that again."

Such behavior demeans others and always produces negative results. A successful couple is sensitive to the needs of others. If discussion is not appropriate at the moment, that fact can be stated without making the other party feel he or she is not to be heard from. "Could we talk about this a little later?" is a perfectly appropriate response on occasion, as long as it's followed up on.

SUPPLYING ANSWERS WHERE NONE ARE NEEDED

The Hopkins family is at dinner, seated around their dining-room table. "It sounds like you're getting a sore throat, Charlene," Kent says to his wife.

"Oh, yes, it's the one you brought home from the office last week," Charlene answers.

"But that was only a runny nose, not—" Kent starts.

"I knew I'd get it in time. Now the kids will, too, and we'll be in for a siege," Charlene says. "With all the people you come in contact with, I'm surprised we're not sick all the time."

Let's stop a moment and look at what's happening here. Charlene is convinced that Kent brought her the sore throat. Kent's statement that he had only a runny nose (he was cut off before he could say he had no sore throat) falls on deaf ears. Charlene has it all figured out; facts only confuse.

How does this leave Kent feeling? Is not the tone somewhat blaming? Would Kent not likely feel it is somehow his fault that he contacts people, some of whom carry sicknesses at any given moment? Whether or not blame is what Charlene intends, Kent could easily receive this message.

There's more to the story. Let's look in on the Hopkins family a few moments later. Thirteen-year-old Bart is speaking:

> "So I don't know if I did very well. It was an awful long test. Nobody finished it."
>
> "You were probably just tired, Bart," Charlene says.
>
> "Tired? Why would I be tired, Mom?" Bart asks.
>
> "Because you've been staying up too late for weeks. I've told you."
>
> Bart shakes his head and resumes eating. "I don't feel tired," he mutters.
>
> "He does stay up late, but he doesn't seem to need as much sleep as our other kids did at the same age," Kent says.
>
> "Kent," Charlene says, "are you saying it's OK for Bart to stay up late? You don't care when a thirteen-year-old goes to bed?"

Here is another case of Charlene's insistence that her explanation is the only appropriate one. No matter that Bart doesn't feel tired or that no one else finished the test either. Charlene just "knows" these things. Here we see her problem more clearly: Charlene supplies answers where none are needed—where, in fact, no questions exist. It's as if she has a need to know where her sore throat came from and why her son didn't do well on his test, so she supplies convenient answers.

Later, the story goes on. Charlene is talking:

> "Marge Blankenship called today about the PTA fund-raiser, Kent. She was on the committee last year. Well, she said she had some ideas I might want to consider for this year."
>
> "What do you have to do with the PTA fund-raiser?" Kent asks.
>
> "You didn't know I'm in charge this year?"
>
> "No."
>
> "Well, you're not around much; I guess I never told you."
>
> Kent hesitates, then says, "Anyway, I guess if Marge is willing to help, that's good, isn't it? You don't usually get volunteers."
>
> "Except," Charlene says, "you know Marge. The only reason she'd offer is to get to do it her way. Oh, I shouldn't say that. She's a hard worker and all. But, well, you know how she is."

Charlene may be an extreme case. But there are people like her. She has a need to see through everything, to provide motives for everyone and reasons for every action. By creating these "facts," she manages to control her life as well as the lives of many of the people around her. Rather than acknowledging her own failure to tell Kent of her assignment, she points out that he isn't around enough to hear about it. Rather than hear Marge's suggestions and choose which to accept, she attributes bad motives to her. Charlene can't be reasoned with; she already "knows" how things are.

Such certainty about people's needs and motives is a

form of control, one guaranteed to produce negative results in a marriage. The fact is, none of Charlene's assertions can be proven. While she certainly has a right to an opinion, her simplistic attitude, her phrasing of things in black-and-white terms, and her certainty about unknowables smack of superstition. If the causes of every effect were this clear and obvious, Charlene would be a sage, a true wisewoman. As it is, she's closer to an opinionated sermonizer who alienates the rational thinkers in her family.

EXORCISE YOUR GHOSTS

"A great meal, Lonette."

"Thanks, Gary," Lonette said.

"I'll say," Gary's wife, Sue, added.

"This pie reminds me of one my mom used to make," Gary said. "Oh," he caught himself, "Sue makes a great pie, too."

Sue laughed. "I'll never match the memory of your mom's pie, Gary. We both know that."

"You have that problem, too, huh?" Lonette said. "I've never been able to make a pot roast like the ones Mac ate growing up."

Mac shrugged. "It's true, but I love you anyway. It's probably a different species of beef nowadays."

"Let's move to the living room, shall we?" Lonette suggested. Gary and Sue sat together on the couch, while Mac and Lonette each took their favorite easy chairs.

"You know, those comments about the pie and the pot roast are interesting," Mac said. "Maybe it's too obvious to talk about, but don't we all bring quite a few things with us from childhood that affect us and our marriages?

"For example, how we look at food is a big one, I think. Not only that we might prefer certain tastes acquired in childhood—mom's potato salad, for example, or salad dressing instead of mayonnaise or vice versa—but how we feel about food, what it means to us.

"I was talking to a young woman at work a few days ago. She's overweight and feels bad about it. She was saying she didn't want to blame anyone, but that, growing up in her house, her mom linked food directly with love. When her mom cooked something—and she was apparently a good cook—it was her way of showing her kids she loved them. Cooking wasn't a duty for her; it was an act of love. So, everybody was expected to partake heartily, very heartily.

"Talking to her started me thinking that we probably all carry around many ideas—mostly unconscious—about what things mean."

"Like birthdays?" Lonette asked.

Mac grinned. "Yeah," he said, "like birthdays." When Gary and Sue waited expectantly, Lonette went on. "See, when we were married, we learned we looked at things like this differently. In my house, birthdays were enormous events, planned weeks in advance, with oodles of presents and parties. Relatives always called or sent cards; some even drove miles to come to a birthday party for us kids.

"We'd been married five months when my birthday came around. Well, it was a major crisis for me when it was no big deal to Mac. I mean, he wished me happy birthday that morning, then we went off to classes. (We were still in college.) I thought, 'Well, he's planning something for later.'

"That night, when we both got home, he did have a present there. It was a blouse I needed.

114

He'd stretched the budget to afford it, and I appreciated it. But as for the image I'd grown up with of what birthdays are supposed to be, forget it! The blouse wasn't wrapped, just there on the table in the bag from the store. There was no card, no dinner invitation, no flowers, no balloons. My folks sent a card and a gift, and called that evening, which kind of salvaged the day.

"So here I was trying to figure this out. All I could think is how Mac didn't really love me. That's how these things seem at times. I guess we're so tied to a certain way of doing things and the meaning of those things, that we don't know how to interpret a new approach. Of course, Mac knew none of this until much, much later. I actually went to sleep like a little kid waiting for Santa: I still thought that any minute Mac would jump up and say 'surprise,' and we'd have a 'real' birthday party."

"I know what you're saying," Sue said. "There are so many of those things. Money is a big one—not only whether or not you have it and how you handle it, but what it means to you—power or security or whatever.

"Lateness is another one. You know, I grew up thinking being late was discourteous—period. Well, is it always? Does it have to mean that? I don't think Gary thinks so."

Gary said, "What about touching? My family are great touchers, always hugging. You could go to the grocery store and come back and get a hug. Sue's family doesn't do that at all. They are these 'arm's-length' types, or 'ten-foot-pole' types. They seemed cold to me at first, like they didn't care about people."

"And," Sue interrupted, "I thought his fam-

115

ily was plain weird. What was all this 'hands-on' stuff, you know?"

What these two couples are talking about is ghosts. Ghosts are ways of looking at things we learned somewhere in the past that come back to haunt and control relationships. As illustrated in Lonette's story of her first birthday after she was married, ghosts can have great emotional impact on people. They can affect how we view virtually everything from church to careers, from the way we vote to the kind of car we drive.

Many of the good things we do are the result of ghosts — positive ways of viewing things we learned in our youth. These help our marriage work. But others may get in the way, may interfere with the relationship.

As mature couples, we can look back, as the two couples in the story are doing, and analyze. But at the time the ghost is in charge, it's no easy matter. The best we can do, at any age or stage of the marriage, is try to understand, put ourselves in the shoes of the other person, and, most of all, talk about our concerns. In these ways, we can recognize, then exorcise, many of the ghosts controlling our relationship.

OWNERSHIP

Guy Wheeler was settled in his favorite armchair in the den. "Laureen," he said, "I'm glad we can talk. I see you're pretty taken by this Tad. You seem to be handling it pretty well — showing maturity and taking things slowly. Projecting too soon how things will turn out can be dangerous, so I hope you're being cautious. You're only nineteen, and you have plenty of time."

"I know, Dad," Laureen said. "But he is by far the neatest guy I've ever gone with."

116

"Exactly what your mom said about me — the neatest 'Guy.' " Guy grinned. Laureen chuckled at her dad's play on words. "Can I make an observation, though, about you and Tad?"

"Sure."

"Let me say it like this. When your mom and I started getting serious, and even when we were first married, I was not the mature, wonderful man you have come to know."

Laureen enjoyed her dad's way of teasing about himself. He went on.

"What I learned — mostly from Deana, after we were married, and after a few real tough times — was that she was a person in her own right. I think I was a typical young male — concerned with showing how macho I was. We didn't use that term then. We called it cool or tough or something. What it meant was that I thought I was in charge of everything — including Deana."

"From what I've heard and read," Laureen said, "that's still pretty typical for males, young ones, anyway."

"Right. But it isn't the ideal. And from what I've seen of Tad, he has the problem to some extent. I know you have long talks, and you've said he understands you and all, but I've noticed he really likes you to do things his way. For example, remember when you were sick a month or so ago, and he told you he wouldn't 'let' you go to class?"

"Yes."

"Well, you said you thought you felt well enough to go, but you went along with his wishes — or commands. My guess — based on my great wisdom and vast years of experience — is

that you felt OK about that. You accepted it from
him—and probably wouldn't have from us, incidentally—because you felt protected, loved,
taken care of. You felt like you were making him
happy. Am I close to correct?"

"Yeah, I think so. It didn't bother me."

"My point is, from what I knew of the incident, he didn't really care what you thought; he
just took charge. Now, as a young girl in love,
you kind of like this. But I also know you're a
very independent person—always have been—
and I wonder whether you'll like such direction
quite as well twenty or thirty years from now—if
you were to marry Tad, I mean.

"See, what I'm saying is that what seems fine
now—since you interpret it as caring—can really
get on your nerves if later you interpret it differently—such as not being sensitive to your
needs."

Laureen was silent, so Guy went on. "Maybe
it's too much to expect most twenty-year-old
young men to be otherwise. Our culture pretty
much teaches males to take charge, after all. But
if you get more serious with Tad, or anybody
else, I hope you'll watch for signs that he's willing to recognize you as a separate person, not a
possession."

Guy raises a fine point, whether or not his daughter
is prepared to hear it: One spouse doesn't own another.
Young people, especially males, don't always act as if they
know this. They're often still discovering themselves and
trying to fit the perceived cultural expectations of their
roles. They usually haven't had enough experience to have
established the point of view we call liberated—some aspects of which are rather subtle.

Phrases about not "letting" or "allowing" spouses to do certain things remind us of serfdom because they show an attitude of ownership. The ideal is partnership, where no permission is needed for a spouse to do what he or she decides is best. The control of one's action lies with each individual, not in the hands of a spouse.

DEMANDING CERTAIN REACTIONS

Lawrence turned off the porch light and started to lock the front door. "Is the cat still out, Barbara?" he called up the stairs.

"No, she's in," his wife answered.

"OK," Lawrence said. He turned out the last downstairs light and came up to the bedroom.

"Well, that turned out nicely," Barbara said. "I'm tired, though."

"Yes, it was fun to see the Appletons again. It's been a long time, and he and I were such good buddies in basic training." Lawrence paused before going on. "You seemed . . . uh, quiet I guess. Subdued or something."

"Oh?" Barbara said. "I guess I was tired. I didn't realize—"

"I decided you didn't really enjoy them," Lawrence said.

"Oh, sure I did, honey. She was very nice, and I enjoyed seeing you two guys go over old times."

"Well, I just wanted you to be more involved somehow," Lawrence said. "But *you* described what I thought: You enjoyed seeing us talk, you said, like you were only an observer. I wanted you to be more a part of the group."

Barbara was puzzled and a little exasperated. "Well, I'm sorry, Lawrence. I don't know what you wanted. I had a good time."

"It's like when I brought home that Mann-
heim Steamroller album last week I thought was
so neat, and you listened and finally said, 'It's
kind of all the same after a while, isn't it?'"

"Well, Lawrence, I didn't realize I was supposed to give any certain response. I enjoyed the
music, but clearly not as much as you did. What
am I supposed to say?"

Lawrence is guilty of one of the most unfair of relationship practices: demanding of his wife specific reactions
to specific events. He doesn't seem to fully accept Barbara's
statement that she had a good time except for being tired.
He's somehow disappointed in her behavior at the gath-
ering. Apparently she was not a "fascinating woman" tonight.

He also expected a more enthusiastic response to the
album he brought home. And while anyone can understand his desire to share with his wife and to see her
interested in those things he likes, Barbara poses a good
question: "What am I supposed to say?"

The options aren't numerous. Is she to lie, to pretend
to like something more than she really does to please her
husband? When does such behavior go beyond courtesy
and become hypocrisy? If she must make a pretense to
please Lawrence, something important in the way of honesty and openly shared feelings has been lost. Well might
Barbara ask if she is to be a real person or merely a robot.

Lawrence's desires amount to controls on his wife, if
she accepts them. Such demands reduce his wife's worth
and diminish the relationship at the cost of making him
something of a despot.

THREATENING THE RELATIONSHIP

"If that's all our marriage means to you . . ."
"I can't live with this situation . . ."

"If you don't value me any more than that, I don't see how we can go on . . . "

These comments have one thing in common: they state a subtle or a direct threat to the relationship. They challenge the other spouse to defend or "prove" his or her love and commitment.

Comments like these remind us of a game couples sometimes play in the early years of dating. It starts with some incident, no matter how slight, that causes jealousy in one of the two. The injured party then displays anger or hurt feelings (pouting is a favorite response) and the other party has to reestablish the relationship. It's a game of forcing a person to show how much he or she really cares.

When this immature game carries over to marriage, it carries the potential for disaster and constitutes an extreme form of control over the relationship. Demands for proving devotion, even when subtle, are examples of harmful negative controls that must be avoided. "If you loved me . . . " requests really mean, "If you do things my way . . . " Like any other "power" game, this one has no end, once begun.

Couples are well advised to avoid mentioning divorce or of talking about how their relationship might end over this or that problem. They will also, incidentally, avoid at all costs physical separations over solitary incidents, no matter how virulent. The exception is in the case of physical violence, threatened or actual. Otherwise, separation as a problem-solving tool must occur only after outside counseling.

The problem of threats is that they are an effort at controlling another person. The danger is that someone may eventually take us up on them. They have no place in marriage.

SHARING EVERYTHING?

Alice laughed into the telephone. "Judith! Good to hear you. I was just sitting here looking

out at this dreary weather when the phone rang.
Reminds me of some of the worst days on the
ranch growing up. You'd remember those better
than I do."

"OK, baby sister. You don't have to remind
me how old I am. When my little sister is fifty-
nine, and I remember the day she was born,
then I know even without your reminders what
an ancient thing I am."

"And how's everything at your place?" Alice
asked.

"Pretty good. But you sound like you have a
frog in your throat."

"Oh, I do. I shouldn't have gone to the ball
game last Saturday. It was so cold. But you know
Calvin—he wouldn't miss a football game if they
had to play it on ice skates."

"You ought to be careful this time of year.
There are lots of nasty things going around. This
is your big sister giving advice now. But hey,
you like those college games as much as Cal does
any day."

"I do not," said Alice.

"What are you telling me?" Judith asked.
"You two have gone to those games for years."

"Not on account of me," Alice said. "I only
go because of Calvin."

"Are you serious?"

"Of course. I hate football."

"You could've fooled me, dear. Does Cal
know this great secret?"

"Certainly. But he made clear that he wants
me to come with him. He hates to go alone. So I
go to support him."

"And I suppose he comes to your reading

club and your quilting sessions to support you,"
Judith said sarcastically.

"I think you know the answer to that," Alice
answered.

How interesting. A woman has spent hours in the heat
and the cold watching an activity she hates—all to support
her husband. Now, on one level, this devoted support is
perhaps very admirable—here is a woman joining her husband in an activity he enjoys more by her presence. Any
spouse will feel a need to join in such activities occasionally.

On another level, this is strange behavior indeed, especially since Alice's support is not reciprocated by Calvin.
It is cruel and unusual punishment to regularly have to sit
in the bleachers at an event that one detests. Why is it
necessary? Why didn't Calvin years ago find friends with
whom he could enjoy his football games? Why, when he
knew his wife disliked the game, did he insist on her
attendance? And why was she unable to feel good about
opting out?

Is simply being with a person showing support? Or is
it, under certain conditions, phony? The demand for everything to be done together in a marriage can become a
burden, a control placed on one spouse by the other. Not
that one person might not learn to enjoy football—and
another quilting. But without that enjoyment, support re-
mains only an outward matter, not a genuine one.

The question of support, and how it's given in marriage, is a big one. Some couples share everything. When
one reads a book, the other reads it too. When one enjoys
football games, the other goes too. They watch TV together, eat breakfast together, go shopping together.

This can be good; it can strengthen a marriage. At least,
it can if both feel good about the activities shared. However, if one feels required to attend activities that aren't
enjoyed, then sharing becomes forced and might not be

so wonderful. Many couples seem to do fine without such close sharing of every event, which can come across as controlling. Spencer W. Kimball, twelfth president of The Church of Jesus Christ of Latter-day Saints, in his younger years took a vacation trip without his wife, Camilla, simply because he wanted to go and she didn't.

This is not a matter of right or wrong, but of style. The difference is in the expectation of what married couples do or should do. If a husband continually drags his wife fishing "for the companionship," and she has no interest at all in the sport, the relationship may be losing more than it is gaining. Her "support" may actually be phony, and she can come to resent it.

People should be free to each develop interests that they pursue alone or with others, without an automatic obligation on the part of the other spouse to become involved.

QUESTIONS FOR DISCUSSION

Does one of us control the agenda so others have no chance to express opinions or make decisions?

Do we find ourselves giving "answers" where none were needed?

Have we identified ghosts and their influence in our marriage?

How are we at allowing one another independent choices?

Do we allow each other to react honestly, or do we pressure for conformity?

Have we avoided threatening our relationship in our arguments? Do either of us feel subtly threatened now?

Do we each have interests not shared by the other? Do either of us place guilt on the other for not giving greater support in specific areas?

CHAPTER 7

WILLINGNESS
TO CHANGE

How easy for most of us to see where others need to change; how tough to accept that it might be us in need of improvement. Oh, in principle, we accept the idea that all of us have a lot of growing to do, but when it comes right down to facing individual problems, we tend to see faults in others more easily than in ourselves.

In a marriage, both parties must send the message that they are willing to improve and grow. And that means being willing to listen to those who would help us, for often a spouse is able to see us more clearly than we could ever see ourselves. In marriages where suggestions for change are reciprocal and properly handled, great growth can occur.

Not only must we be willing to change when problems are brought to our attention, but we must seek information about how we're doing. An observing spouse in a comfortable, supportive relationship can be the best friend we'll ever have in helping us see ourselves.

Change may involve effort and pain. It may also become tiresome, since the process continues throughout life. We never reach a stopping point, because each time we arrive at a new plateau, we can see new, higher peaks ahead. But while it's tough to pursue a path with only an upward slope, it's worthwhile. What can be of more value to us in the long run than to become more fulfilled people and better marriage partners?

In this chapter, couples will look at attitudes and approaches—and especially at willingness—to change.

"THAT'S JUST HOW I AM."

"Well, today is our last meeting," Sister Myers said. "The twelve weeks have gone quickly, and I've enjoyed teaching this family relations class every Sunday. I hope it's been helpful to you as couples.

"Now, last week I asked you to be prepared to share with us a final suggestion or two from your own experience that has helped in your relationship. Who'd like to be first?"

After a pause, Sister Myers said, "Sister Conklin, why don't you start us off? I'll bet you have something to share."

A small, middle-aged woman rose from her seat. "Well, Morris isn't in here," she said. "He's substituting in a youth class this morning. But he and I talked about something we might say today. During the past few years, we've used a concept in our marriage and with our kids that's become our family philosophy, I guess. It's very simple: Nobody in our family is allowed to use the phrase, 'That's just how I am.'

"I think it started when we would try to get our kids to stop a poor behavior or start a new one, and our teenagers, as they got older, would state some form of, 'Hey, Mom, that's just how I am. Dig?'

"Well, one day a few years ago, Morris and I were talking to one of the kids about something. We got that response, and I said, 'I don't like that. It sounds like people can't change.' And I told a story of a college professor I once had who always said, 'If you want to feel better, do better.'

"Over the years, since that discussion, this idea has evolved a little at our house, and we now say, 'OK, I accept that's how you are. Now, what will you become, starting today?'

"It was some time later before Morris and I started to see how we used the same kind of excuse in our marriage, but in different words. It wasn't only our kids who said 'That's how I am.' We had our phrases, too, like 'I tried,' and 'You always see only faults,' and 'You do the same thing,' all phrases that shifted the problem to the other spouse.

"We made a decision that those would not be acceptable answers in our discussions, and it has made a great difference in our marriage."

The Conklins recognize the danger of falling back on slippery excuses like "That's just how I am." When a person makes such a statement, he or she is denying the power of change, of improvement—of repentance, if you will. We can all change.

This couple has hit upon a philosophical approach of value. They accept how they are, but they move on from there: "That's how you are. Fine. Now, what will you become?"

We may not hide behind the generality that all of us fall short; we must be willing to improve. If each time we're confronted with a shortcoming, we fall back on the "I'm-not-perfect" excuse, we deny ourselves the chance to learn what the specific problem is and to make improvements to change it. None of us is perfect, but saying so can become an excuse, a shield by which we knock away the ministering hands of one whom we perceive to be the enemy, but who is actually the physician.

LOOKING FOR FEEDBACK

The gray-haired man pushed himself back from the table and stood, tapping on the side of his glass with a fork. "I suppose you all wonder why I've called you here," Parley Despain said, chuckling at the old cliché. The visiting subsided in the small room as attention was focused on him.

"Of course, first, it was to eat, and I hope you've had all you want. Mom and I talked pretty hard to get the restaurant people to let us use this room to eat in and then to meet in for a few minutes afterward, so we'd better get started.

"I warned you when we invited you to dinner that I had something I wanted to present to you—our married children and spouses. Now that we've arranged to get all of you away from the kids for a few minutes, and bribed you with dinner, let me present to you what Mom and I have in mind."

Parley sat down again. "Now that I've got your attention, I'm going to sit down, where Mom can more easily poke me in the ribs if I go on too long.

"The subject is probably going to surprise you that we would dare to mention it. It's about your marriages. Now, I need to say some things right at the start. First, your marriages are your business. We have no intention of prying or asking questions in any form. Second, we aren't bringing up this subject because of concerns about any of you. Your years of marriage range from about twenty-seven down to fourteen, I think, so none of you are newlyweds. If any of you happen to be having any particular problems with your relationship right now, we don't know about it—or need to. So, please, don't read any more into this meeting than just a little old-fogey parental advice. OK?"

Before anyone could answer, Laurel, Parley's wife, said, "They're plenty used to that by now."

"Right," Parley said dryly. "So here we go. Let me start with an incident that happened in our marriage many, many years ago. Laurel was being, I thought, particularly tough on me about something. I've honestly forgotten the issue, but I remember the feeling. Finally, I exploded at her, 'Why are you after me all the time?'

"That got her upset, and we had words. When we calmed down and talked it through, she said something to me I've never forgotten. It was to the effect that, in spite of my working in church callings and being around lots of people at the office and so forth, she was probably the only person in the whole world who could or would give me really honest feedback.

"Of course it was true, and obvious as soon as she said it, but still a revolutionary idea to me. So I'm going to repeat it for you: Your spouse is really the only one who is likely to bother to help you do better. Most others will usually tolerate your foibles and not make it their business.

"Not to say that spouses don't learn to tolerate a lot, too, and let many things go by, but if it's something crucial, there's no one in a better position to help you than your wife or husband. They're with you enough to see the patterns in your behavior. And they care enough about you to help. This puts them in a position of perhaps being 'hard on you,' but it's sometimes necessary. I hope you're all to the point in your marriages where you can help each other—and where you can accept help without animosity.

"Now, with that introduction, what we propose today is to pass out a sheet of ideas I came across. You can use it as you will—toss it out if you want to. But we encourage you to use this or some other process of talking and growing together and establishing a framework for giving proper feedback to one another. Let's read through the page and then I'm through. We can order dessert and go home."

Parley has taken a courageous step in talking candidly with his grown children about the marriage relationship and a willingness to grow and change. He's quite right in not interfering in any of the specifics of his children's marriages, but he can't be blamed for his interest.

Parley's central idea is vital. There simply is no one else in a position of such close observation and interest in our growth as our spouse. Surely we must find ways to help one another and to accept that help. Nor is the spouse to be blamed if the prescribed cure is a hard one; some ailments are hard to remedy, but that's not the fault of the doctor.

Parley's sheet of ideas for discussion is instructive. They include the following:

—How important is it to see myself as I really am? In little things? In big things? In things that affect others, especially the family?

—How accepting am I of the idea that I must change and grow and not just sit where I am?

—Do I agree that good people can have harmful, self-protecting, ego-laden traits? That not being able to see oneself clearly in all situations does not equate with "badness" as a person?

—Do I agree that innocently intended behavior can sometimes produce negative results? That I must be willing to change the behavior, in spite of its innocence, to improve the outcome?

—Do I believe that my spouse might be able to see me more clearly than I see myself?

—Do I agree to accept criticism given in love and not see it as an accusation of bad motives?

—Am I willing to ask my spouse to tell me how I come across? Will I reciprocate?

—Am I willing to work out a plan with my spouse for regular feedback and discussion?

These constitute a beginning list for a relationship based on mutual feedback and a willingness to grow.

CHANGE IS PAINFUL

Thomas sat on a bench in the backyard, out of direct sight of the house. He was over his worst anger. Now his feeling was one of amazement at how things had gone this morning. It was Saturday, and they had all been a little lazy getting up. As he was finishing his French toast with DeAnn, she suddenly stood and said, "Oh, no!"

"Good heavens, what is it?" Thomas asked in alarm.

"Oh," DeAnn said. "I just can't believe it. I entirely forgot to type a paper for Amelia."

When Thomas looked blank, DeAnn went on. "She's taking a night class, and she's so busy with her family and work, and I offered to type her final draft for her. She gave me the paper Wednesday, and I told her I'd do it by last night. She wanted to take it to a study group this morning for critique. Maybe I can still finish. Oh, I don't know. It's probably too late. I'll have to call and see."

Thomas wondered why DeAnn took things so hard. Amelia would understand. Then came the problem. As DeAnn stood to reach for the phone, she said, "Gee!" It was a word that seemed filled with anger and disgust at herself. The intensity made Thomas shake his head and breathe softly, "Gee."

The response was instantaneous. "Don't make fun of me!" DeAnn said indignantly.

"I wasn't making fun of you," Thomas said. "I . . . "

By then DeAnn had turned and was dialing the phone. Thomas left the table.

As he now thought about it, he tried to analyze what his "Gee" had meant. He felt that his reaction was because of DeAnn's intense desire to look good with neighbors or others outside the home. Just the night before, when she'd told him that one of the Scouts in his troop had called, she said, "Be sure to call back or you make me look bad."

This happened so often—this fear of losing face outside the home—that Thomas found it incredible that DeAnn couldn't see how extreme she was with it. Yet he noticed no such anxiety within the family. For example, when DeAnn forgot, last week, to pick up his pants from the cleaners after she'd said she would, she dismissed it with, "Well, I just forgot. I can get them tomorrow, can't I?" Only outsiders drove her to anxiety.

But she didn't accept Thomas's views on this matter. She rejected the idea that she was overly worried about outsiders. Thomas had brought up the problem a dozen times over the years, always sensing total rejection. There was never even any interest in hearing the evidence. This time, he decided, he wouldn't even bother to mention it again.

If Thomas is right—and admittedly we've heard only his side of the story—DeAnn may have a problem. If she's really been presented with evidence "a dozen times,"—and if the evidence has been presented in a helpful, noncombative way—DeAnn is under obligation to examine it.

On the other hand, Thomas can ask himself why this issue bothers him so much. So what if his wife happens to be more concerned than he with peer recognition? Is it a big thing? As is often the case, this negative trait may be merely the dark side to a positive quality in DeAnn—her outgoing and sociable nature.

Thomas needs to distinguish between mere differences in personality—which may be irritating, yet still harmless—and actual problems. Before asking his wife to change, he must ask himself if he is the one needing the alteration. If the problem is more in his own mind than in reality, it might be his own attitude that needs adjustment.

HOW WE THINK

"Now for those of you who've been waiting to call in and ask Dr. Matthew Flammer a specific question or get his advice on an aspect of your relationship, you'll have a chance to do so right after this message."

While the commercial played, the announcer explained to Dr. Flammer how to handle his headset so as to hear the incoming calls. The spot ended and the first call came in.

"Good morning, do you have a question or comment for Dr. Flammer?"

"Yes, I do," a female voice said. "I don't want to blame my husband, because I know there are two sides to everything, but we have a problem. Without giving all the details, it's basically money. We simply can't get together on spending or saving or anything.

"I can accept people having differing views about money. We've talked about it, and we realize I was raised one way and he another. But he says he wants to be more careful and not to buy everything he sees, and then he'll come with a new shotgun—his 'old' one was three years old—or, the other day, new seat covers for the car—which we didn't need at all.

"When I have a fit about these things, which I'll admit I sometimes do, he'll say, 'Well, this was on sale,' or 'Oh, they weren't that expensive.' Sometimes I can get him to take things back, though not usually. We're supposed to be saving for a house, and it's discouraging."

Dr. Flammer said, "I can tell it is, and that's understandable. You realize I can't give you a simple solution that will work in all cases. In many marriages, money is a tough issue. Money itself is psychologically complex; it's loaded with meanings and overtones. And as you pointed out, I've only heard one side of the story, so I won't take sides here. OK?"

"Sure, I understand."

"What I can do," Dr. Flammer said, "is to give a few principles that might help—not only with money, but with any problem.

"First, people don't always see themselves as others see them. But in any discussion, there must be acceptance of the idea that what people do tends to reflect what they believe. We are

what we think. There are reasons for what we
do. Not that we can always identify the reason,
but accepting that idea helps us stop rationaliz-
ing.

"The sale price doesn't make anyone buy anything. It only gives an impetus, a defense, an excuse. So the first principle is this: People need to
accept the fact that their thinking, their way of
seeing things, controls their actions. Each instance of behavior may be explained away, but if
a pattern exists, that pattern comes from our
thinking, not from outside sources. Are you with
me so far?"

"Yes, I think so."

"This idea is very important so people don't
blame outside influences for their own decisions.
OK. Now, when we look at behavior patterns to
try to find the thinking behind them, we're not
merely trying to show a person all their mistakes.
It's a different motive entirely."

"Sometimes my husband thinks I'm picking
on him."

"It's important that you know in your own
heart that's not your intent, and that he know
you are trying to show him a pattern he has.
Then he needn't feel attacked or hurt. He doesn't
have to feel he is being asked to change for your
sake, but for his own.

"If you can both come to terms with that—
that you are asking him to examine his way of
thinking not for you but for himself or for the
family—there's a chance of change. And when it
occurs, it will be, in part, because he's accepted
the idea that the patterns of his behavior reveal
the real him, and he wants to become a different
person."

Dr. Flammer reminds us of how we reveal ourselves through the things we do. If we regularly fritter away money while stating that we want to save, at some level we must really want to fritter. We may explain each expenditure as a "bargain," but we need only realize that other shoppers refrained from buying to know that it is still our own desire that "made" us buy.

If we regularly overeat while alleging that we're dieting, we reveal that, somewhere within us, we choose to eat. While hunger may be perfectly understandable, it's not a reasonable excuse to say, "The pie just looked so good, I couldn't resist." We've all said such things; let's just not really believe them!

We are not cows or other semiconscious creatures merely reacting to our environment, even though some try to defend their actions by saying they have no control over them; they are just "overcome."

Not quite. We are thinking, choosing, intelligent agents; we do what we want to do; we are what we think. Change what I think and you have changed me.

When couples are serious about their desire to change and improve, they will be willing to let spouses help them see the patterns of their behavior. They will accept what these patterns reveal about their thinking. Then, as their thinking reveals their real selves, they can decide if and how they wish to change.

UNWILLINGNESS TO SEE LOGICAL CONCLUSIONS

JoAnn and Wynn sat in the family car in their driveway, the only place they could talk without being disturbed by the children.

"So," JoAnn was saying, "I feel bad when you and Cindy have these run-ins. I'm not blaming you, you know; I only wish there were a way to reduce the hostility."

"She shows no respect. I won't let her get

away with talking that way. I don't care if she is nearly seventeen."

"She's got a mean mouth, all right," JoAnn said. "But we've talked to her about it so many times, and she still doesn't change. I wonder if there isn't some other approach. Since this is primarily between you and her, maybe if you responded differently . . . "

"How can I, when she talks back like that? I won't tolerate it," Wynn protested.

"Well, all I'm saying, Wynn, is that she isn't mature enough to realize the consequences, but you and I need to look ahead at what the results will be if this continues. I think she's getting further away from us all the time."

"Yes, she is."

"And if it continues, where will it lead? If she's alienated enough, she's old enough to think she can take off on her own, and she's too young to handle the world out there . . . "

"I guess it's her choice. If she's going to talk like that, I just can't respond any other way. I'm sorry, JoAnn, but that's the way I feel."

Wynn isn't willing to look at the actual consequences of continued problems between himself and his daughter. He won't follow his wife's thinking through to its logical conclusion. "I just can't respond any other way," he says.

Of course, he's wrong. He can respond any way he chooses. But his attitude is one of not wanting to see where he might be at fault, and where he could change. As a parent and as a spouse, he is weakened by his unwillingness to recognize and see ahead.

How often we fail to see where our actions will lead us. Whether intentional or not, an unwillingness to look ahead is based on fear. Fortunately, others—including spouses—can help, if they're allowed. Part of a spouse's job includes looking at his or her partner's actions and talking together about where the behavior is leading in the relationship or the family. It's like helping the blind to see, and we're all blind on certain subjects. Who among the sightless would not accept the gift of vision?

ONE TRAIT CHANGES EVERYTHING

It was a beautiful morning. The snow-capped mountain peaks glistened in the bright sun.

"Isn't that gorgeous?" Merle asked. "The lake is as smooth as marble this early in the day. I'm glad we could come up here with you."

Michelle sat beside her mom on the dock watching the two figures in the fishing boat on the far side of the small lake. She didn't answer until Merle looked her way.

"Oh," she said. "Yes, Mom, it really is beautiful. Sorry. I was drifting somewhere."

The two women were silent for another moment. Finally Michelle said, "I apologize for the little scene here a few moments ago, too. That's what I was thinking about. I guess Rex and I aren't always on our best behavior, even when you and Dad are around."

"No apologies necessary, Michelle. Your dad and I weren't always on our best behavior when we were raising you either! These things happen."

"Oh, I know," Michelle said, "But I still hate it. I expect a certain number of problems in marriage. What I didn't know about is all the unpredictables. I mean, how would I know that sleeping in a little this morning would be the end of the world? I thought we were on vacation. But to Rex, getting out on the lake by sunup was suddenly vital, and he sure got snappy when breakfast wasn't ready when he thought it ought to be."

Merle didn't comment on the specifics. "Well, we'll know better tomorrow, won't we? Look, one of them is pulling in something right now. I can't tell whether it's Rex or Daddy, but if they keep that up, they'll come back in a fine mood."

Michelle gazed off toward the top of the peak across the lake. "I've never seen Dad be that way to you, Mom," she said quietly.

"Mostly because you were too young to notice and because you have a selective memory, dear. We both did our share of snapping. Still do, occasionally.

"We've gotten a lot better at not being bothered by the little things. Incidentally, in case you think I'm bragging, I read something the other day that amazed me. I'd always assumed people finally learned to do better as they aged and matured. But then I read that we lose part of our fieriness as we get older because some of our brain cells die every day! This mellows our responses."

"Oh, great," Michelle laughed. "You mean I have to wait until I'm half brain-dead before I'll be a nicer person?"

"Well, I'm not about to accept that as the full story," Merle said. "I'm convinced that we learn, too. There's one thing I learned a few years back that helped a lot: often, one single trait makes a huge difference. If we can see the patterns of what we disagree on, and then isolate just one tendency, it can help a lot.

"For example, I used to be one who always had to keep busy. If I had sat down on this dock to look at the lake—which was unlikely since I'd have probably felt I had to be back in the motor home cleaning—I would have been writing a letter or knitting or something. I felt guilty if I wasn't working—even on vacation.

"Somewhere along the way, I recognized this trait, and I decided I was missing out on some things—my kids, for one. By seeing that one thing and by deciding I would change—worry less about filling every minute—I gradually became a more contented person."

She laughed. "Maybe it was just part of my brain dying, I don't know. But I think one trait sometimes affects so much of what we do, that great improvement can come from working on one specific at a time."

Merle learned a great lesson. One trait can pervade a great deal of what we touch. Like a cook who discovers that he uses too much salt, making one change can make a big difference in the outcome of many dishes. He isn't a bad cook. He just uses too much salt—a specific, reparable item that happens to affect nearly every dish he prepares.

When we become discouraged by our faults or by problems with our spouses, we ought to consider identifying and concentrating on the central trait causing the problem. If the trait is in us, we can try to change it, first by admitting the problem and then by asking for help as necessary. If the fault happens to be in our spouse, we have a choice. We can find ways of helping him or her see it, or we can change our thinking about the problem so that it bothers us less—or both.

Temper, nagging, unrealistic expectations—these and many more traits can cause numerous problems in a relationship. The sheer frequency of the problems may make the situation appear hopeless until we locate and alter the central trait causing the difficulties. Seeing how so many problems disappear when we work on the single trait can be quite encouraging.

Positive traits can also affect things a great deal. Cheerfulness, optimism, kindliness, listening before judging, giving compliments — these are examples of positive traits that can make things much more pleasant all across a relationship.

GUARDING THE "REALM"

Eileen and Gil sat on their patio, enjoying the sunset. "Lamar really got to me today at work," Gil said.

"Oh? What happened?" Eileen asked.

"Nothing so different I guess, just more of the same and sort of the last straw. You remember that the accounts were reshuffled a couple of months ago. Well, I now have several that belonged to him before. And he can't keep his nose out of them. He's always dropping in and asking 'How's Grumwald coming?' or 'Have you followed up with Simmons and Lyon?' It's irritating. He's not my boss."

"You should tell him," Eileen suggested.

"I suppose so." Gil petted the family dog at his feet. "It got me thinking, though, how territorial we are. I notice how someone coming into my office and leaning on my desk can sometimes set me on edge, if they're strangers and kind of act like they're taking over the place, like some people do when they don't respect my 'space.' There's a real feeling of 'guarding my realm' or something. Well, it got me looking at our situation at home."

"In what way?"

"Well, you remember our discussion a while back about things like grocery shopping and food storage."

"Yes, I remember, all right," Eileen said. She recalled clearly feeling that Gil had attacked her procedures.

"Well," Gil said, "I wonder if we haven't made a habit of guarding our own realms so no one can give suggestions. I'm not accusing—I'm sure I do it, too. I'm just exploring an idea."

"OK," Eileen said cautiously. "I'm listening."

"Well, that's about it. I'm in favor of knowing who's in charge of what. I don't want to take over the shopping any more than you want to take over maintaining the cars. But I think we could find ways to listen to each other and consider suggestions—even in those areas we feel most responsible for—like I hope Lamar will, when I talk to him tomorrow."

It's rather automatic to feel intruded upon when someone makes comments about our work or our areas of responsibility. By recognizing this tendency to defend, Eileen and Gil may learn to listen to one another.

If we develop an authentic attitude of being willing to change and improve, we will consider comments even about the areas we feel most responsible for, as well as about the areas mattering little to us. We will guard against defensive reactions that tell the other person that our realm is not to be threatened.

Some are so busy singing "I Did It My Way" that they block out expert help that may be as close as their spouse. There are better lyrics for marriage partners to sing.

ACCEPTING SELF

"What's this, honey?" Eric asked. He held in his hand a sheet of paper labeled "GOALS" he'd picked up from Janet's night stand.

"That's my new goal list," his wife said. "When I decided to go back and finish my degree, I knew I'd have to get better organized, and I came up with this."

"Oh?" Eric said. "I don't know anyone more organized than you already." He scanned the page. " 'A's in all classes,' 'exercise half-hour daily,' 'lose 15 pounds,' 'finish reading New Testament by March,' 'house cleaned before class each day,' 'up at 5 a.m.'

"A pretty hefty list, Janet. I guess I assumed, when we talked about your going back to school, that you'd be cutting things out, not adding more."

"You know what they say," Janet said. "The more you do, the more you can do."

"Is that what 'they' say?"

"Dorothy Harkness told me that when she went back to school, she got straight A's."

"Sure. It can be done. Remember, Dorothy's kids were grown, though, and she doesn't teach piano lessons — which, I notice, are still on your list, too."

"Yes, but I think I can do it. And that is only the list of activities. The back has a list of traits I want to work on. I've got to get some of these things internalized. It's time to do some of these things."

Eric flipped the page over and read aloud a few items from the long list: " 'compassion,' 'patience,' 'time with kids.' " He looked at his wife.

"What do you think?" Janet asked.

"I think either you or the rest of us won't survive this degree."

Perfection. What an enticing goal. But there is a need for balance, for wisdom, for realizing that we really, definitely, and certainly will not become perfect in this life.

Who's to determine a proper balance for how much can be accomplished? For one person, going back to college would be sufficient for the moment. For another, more might comfortably be done in addition. But reason dictates that everything has a price. For every goal, we must ask if the attainment is worth the cost.

Ironically, if Janet is a perfectionist in her demands, and not simply a compulsive goal-setter, her attaining all of the items on her list will not satisfy her. Perfectionists are never satisfied. She will find a new, bigger list to make herself more miserable. How unfortunate that perfectionism causes people to look more closely at their faults than at their strengths.

If Janet could better analyze the big picture, she could see she is already accomplishing a great deal. Adding more might put tremendous pressure on herself and on her husband and family. Each period of life may call for a slightly different balance. Perhaps while going back to school, Janet simply cannot realistically worry about so many other details.

Solutions to perfectionistic attitudes—which may be psychologically deep-seated—don't come easily. But in our desires to change and improve, we must try to be realistic in the goals we set and be willing to accept ourselves as we are.

MAKE YOURSELF A BETTER SPOUSE

Kirsten was surprised to find a personal letter in the batch of business mail left at her desk at the bank. The envelope was marked "Kirsten Hall Rowley—Personal." Even before she saw the return address, she recognized her dad's scrawling handwriting.

"Why would he write me at work instead of at home?" she wondered, as she ran the letter opener along the top edge. She smiled at the first

words on the single sheet of lined paper with
writing on both sides: "OK, so you wonder why
I wrote you at work, instead of at home. I guess
I wanted you to have a chance to read this letter
before you showed it to Vernon."

She settled down to read.

"Kirsten, you know how disappointed I was
that we never got a chance to have one more
good in-depth talk before your marriage. And
now, two months have already gone by. You've
set up housekeeping and gotten settled in your
apartment, and hopefully all is going well. I miss
you a great deal."

Kirsten reflected on the last several years
when she was her father's closest companion
after the death of her mother. She read on.

"I recognize that you are no longer part of
my household, so I hope you won't resent my
giving you a little advice. You are, of course, free
to reject it or tell me to mind my own business.
But you won't, I'll bet—you'll indulge me my pa-
ternal right to preach a little.

"Now that 'the honeymoon is over,' as they
say, you both will start to see things in one another—small and large things—you never knew
before. Each of you will also learn a great deal
about yourselves in your new setting that you
didn't suspect before. Some of these things will
be wonderfully enlightening and delightful. Others will be unbelievably discouraging. And here's
my hope: that you will both nurture the attitude
that you want to grow, to learn, to improve, not
to hold too tightly to your own ways of doing
things to the exclusion of valuing other ways. An
attitude of growth and change will carry you
both a long way. But here's one major caution: In

145

your desire to communicate, state your feelings, and help one another grow. Try to worry less about making your spouse better than about making yourself a better spouse."

Good advice. Of course, working on self first doesn't negate our obligation to help others see themselves. But it's sound direction to keep us on an even keel. Without it, we may tilt too far toward seeing only the problems in others and coming to believe it to be our task to straighten out the world. We will serve ourselves, our spouses, our families, and the world better if we will exert the energy to straighten ourselves out first. The medicine may be bitter, but being healed is worth it.

QUESTIONS FOR DISCUSSION

Do we hide behind excuses like "That's just how I am"? How are we at accepting our present weaknesses while still expecting and working toward growth and change for the future?

Do we want to grow? Are we willing to request and accept feedback and observations from each other?

Are we willing to look at the evidence presented about our poor behavior even when painful?

Are we willing to change our thinking when a pattern of behavior has been revealed to us?

How willing are we to learn from one another about the logical consequences of our behavior?

Are we able to isolate and eliminate individual negative traits that influence so much of what we do? Can we select positive traits to work on?

How are we at accepting comments about domains we are responsible for rather than guarding our realms? How could we be more open to one another in these areas?

Do either of us have perfectionistic trends that make goal-setting and attainments less fulfilling and realistic than they should be?

Individually, are we committed to making ourselves better people first before demanding it of others?

INDEX

"Realm," guarding one's, 141-42
Responses. *See* Answers
Responsibility for relationship: courtship, 85-86; giving priority to marriage, 86-88; talking about relationship, 88-91; commitment, 91-94; loyalty, 94-96; willingness to give, 96-98; sacrifice, 98-101; goals and plans, 101-2; unity and identity, 103-5; responsibility for self, 105-6; questions about responsibility, 106-7; threatening the relationship, 120-21
Roles, defining, 29-32, 96-98
Rules, ground, 60-64

Sacrifice: willingness to make, 96-98; of bad habits, 98-100; too much, 100-101
Schedules. *See* Planning
Scrabble, couple who argued over, 72-73
Self, change in, 125-27, 144-46
Self-responsibility, 105-6
Sharing, 96-98, 121-24
Spouses: images of, 40-43; accepting help from, 125, 128-31, 136-38, 141-42
Support, 32-34, 48-50, 121-24
Surprises in marriage, 2-5

Talk. *See* Communication

Temple trip, miscommunication about, 34-36
Thought affects behavior, 133-36
Threats, 120-21
Time, use of. *See* Planning
Timing, 78-79
Touching, viewpoints about, 115-16
Traits underlying behavior, 138-41

Unity, 103-5

Viewpoints, differing, examples of: birthday party, 1-2; writing a letter, 2-4, 70-72; marriage enrichment seminar, 8-10; closeness, 27-29; child-rearing, 50-51; forgetfulness, 79-80; woman who left family, 100-101; learned attitudes from the past, 113-16; ownership of spouse, 116-18; looking good to others, 131-33; money management, 133-36

Willingness: to sacrifice, 96-100; to make changes, 125-27, 144-46
Winning, costs of, 79-81
Work: husband who is late from, 74-76; using, as excuse, 96-98; couple who planned for change of, 101-3